Contents

Acknowledgements v

Introduction vi

Chapter 1 1
So You Have an Idea for A Television Program—Now What?

Chapter 2 13
Drawing the Blueprint—The Television Proposal

Chapter 3 47
Do the Hustle—Where to Find Financing

Chapter 4 67
Finding the Holy Grail—What to do When the Money Comes In

Chapter 5 82
How to Make More Money—Marketing and Distribution

Chapter 6 102
How to Fake it in TV

Chapter 7 106
Case Studies

Chapter 8 144
Finance Reference Guide
    Canadian National Television Broadcasters........................ 150
    Canadian Provincial Television Broadcasters
       & Provincial Funding Agencies 157
    National Funding Bodies 179

Interim Financing 189
Foreign Broadcasters 193
American Broadcasters 224

Chapter 9 230
Resource Materials Guide

Index 238

Acknowledgements

Every good book is formed by those who helped shape it. A heartfelt thank you to Karen O'Donnell, Dorothy Cumming, Craig Barrett and Claire Sharpe for helping to make this book a reality when there seemed so many obstacles. Thanks to Richard Landau for all his editing pointers, Gail Adams for advice and to Eliza Haddad who helped with information. Much gratitude to those who read drafts, offered suggestions, and took part in case studies. Lastly, thanks to Jean-Christophe who always believes in me and never lets me down. This book is for anyone who has a dream and never gives up.

Introduction

Television. It's an interesting medium isn't it? It gives us reality and fiction and everything in between. I can understand why many people are drawn to it, it seems like a fascinating, exciting business. I was drawn to it too. I used to watch a lot of television when I was young. Eventually I became a television producer and the information I learned (some of it the hard way) makes up the basis of this book.

There are many people who would like to make television programs by becoming producers. People who have an idea for a program and want to see it on the screen so others can enjoy it. Sometimes producing can be an interesting experience but more often than not it involves being stuck in the middle of a lot of paperwork.

Like salespeople, producers have to constantly sell themselves and their programs and unfortunately they are often turned down more than they get accepted. Television is a business where there are no quick returns so you have to have patience. You also have to have a thick skin to be a producer as there are many roadblocks along the way.

There is good news however, communications and the entertainment business are frequently listed as two large growth areas for the future. With the explosion of new specialty channels around the world, as well as satellite television, internet broadcasting, and a whole host of new forms of television yet to be invented, there will always be a demand for television programming. And it takes producers to make programs.

Be cautious, I don't want to make it sound like there is a whole world of broadcasters waiting to beat down your door for programming and everything will be so easy. As you will understand, raising financing for television can be very difficult. Even though the time might be ripe for new programming, the challenge for producers is to get their proposals to the right funding bodies, and telecasters, at the right time. This rings true for new producers as well as experienced producers, the name of the game is to try and find investors to put together the jigsaw puzzle of your financing.

This book is for those who are interested in television and want to become producers or those who are currently producing for television. Sometimes I describe this book as a hybrid because it's really two books in one. The first half is a "how-to" guide for new and emerging producers on how to deal with the business end of producing. It deals with subjects such as how to write a proposal, and how to find financing, two key steps to becoming a producer. The second half of the book is a reference guide for everyone in the television industry from experienced producers, to television broadcasters, as it lists places to find financing for television programs, which is the main task for every producer.

Financing is the most important part of a producer's job because to make a television program it takes thousands of dollars and you have to find that money before you can make your program. Let me tell you, finding money is not easy.

It takes a lot of hard work, patience and tenacity. Bringing entertainment to the masses is no longer only a creative process, it's a financial process as well, filled with business dealings and it's the producer who has a solid grasp of the business side of television, who will get their project off the ground.

I thought of the idea for this book one day while working for a television network. I often dealt with independent producers and was frequently given the task of helping new producers with their program ideas. One fact I realized was that most of them were not very good at articulating their ideas on paper and they had little or no knowledge of how to find financing. I have always believed that if these newer folks were given help with the business end, they could be making wonderful Canadian programming. Let's face it, there is a lot of sub-standard stuff on television and we could use some fresh people with new ideas.

I looked around for reference books to refer them to and realized there weren't many. I also realized there was no central area where all the information about Canadian television financing could be found. So I began compiling this information myself.

I have given much thought to the advice I have provided you with and many of the tips are mine as well as others who have provided antidotes about their experiences in the television industry. Of course you are welcome to follow my advice, or go your own way. Since every television program is different, and every situation is different, you will have to trust your own instincts by following the method of fundraising and writing proposals you feel most comfortable with.

I have made every effort to be accurate and to give you the correct information. If there are any errors, it is purely the fault of the author who apologizes profusely in advance.

Chapter One

*So You Have an Idea for A Television Program—
Now What ?*

Congratulations! You are probably reading this book because you have thought up a wonderful idea for a television program or series and are now searching for the money to produce it. Or you are currently producing projects for television and are flipping through these pages to find new sources of financing. In the first scenario I say congratulations because it takes a certain type of person to think up an idea for a television program; not everyone is blessed with such creativity. In the second scenario I say congratulations because if you've gotten this far you deserve a lot of credit.

There are generally three categories of people in the entertainment industry: the technical craftspeople (or crew), the creative people and the business people. Sometimes it's hard for someone from one of these groups to cross over into another. For example, someone may be great at knowing how to raise money for a production but lousy at thinking up a story idea. Or, as often is the case, someone may have a great story idea but be hopeless at raising funds. In order to be really successful at producing, you have to be good in all three areas: technical, creative and business.

*Three Categories of
People in the
Entertainment
Industry*

Business and Creative Aspects

This chapter will give you a brief outline of the business and creative aspects of producing but will not dwell on the technical or production aspects. There are many fine books already written on those subjects, and as long as you hire an experienced crew, you will ensure that the production looks and sounds great. I often think the golden rule of producing should be "If you don't know how to do it yourself, hire someone who does."

Program or Series Idea

This chapter will also give you the chance to look at your program or series idea closely to see if it has real potential. This is something every producer should do objectively rather than putting a lot of effort into a project that won't get off the ground. It's better to put some thought and a little research into the idea at the beginning to help ensure a fully funded project.

The Business Aspects

The major area of business a producer has to deal with is fundraising. Two of the most common complaints I hear from producers are: "I hate looking for money, I just want to make the program" and "I spend the most time on paperwork and the least on filming."

Fundraising

Fundraising can be fraught with frustration. Filling out application forms, writing proposals, and waiting for investors to respond can be a very tedious and time-consuming job if you're a creative type, but it's the most important building block of your project. Without funding, there will be no program.

Some producers self-finance their production with their own money or by using lines of credit. I have talked to producers who financed their projects by charging all costs of production to their personal credit cards. Some producers even mortgage everything they own to make the project. Self-financing is the most expedient way to get the production going but it makes the least sense; if you can use someone else's money, then why shouldn't you? It's an excellent hedge against potential personal bankruptcy and credit card defaults.

Self-financing

This doesn't mean that all the money you will attract to the production is 'free money,' with no obligation to pay the investment back. Some types of investments require the producer to pay part or all of the money back. In what-ever form the financing comes, it is still money that does not come from your pocket or put your welfare at risk, so doing the paperwork is well worth it.

If you have previously tried doing the financing yourself and really dislike it, try to find a partner who is good at it. The most successful partnerships are the ones in which the partners are complementary to one another. This sort of partnership is often beneficial financially as well; while the creative partner is out filming the current project, the business partner can complete the paperwork on a new project. This method also keeps a steady stream of work in the pipeline.

The Importance of
Partnerships

The other business area that a producer is responsible for is the writing of the program or series idea into proposal format. Fear not; for most people the proposal is not as difficult as the fundraising. It is a document that usually includes a story synopsis, story treatment, budget, finance plan, production schedule and the resume of the producer.

The Creative Aspects

So let's get back to the program or series idea. As the producer, you need to analyze your story idea to see if it can be realistically accomplished and if you will be able to find investors. By investors I mean any combination of funding bodies, public or private, or any other funding scenario you can come up with.

First, you must look critically at your idea and ask yourself the two most important questions: "Is this an idea that will appeal to investors?" and "Will I be able to find a broadcaster to air the program?" Be brutally honest with yourself. It's a natural tendency to fall in love with your own idea. Fight the tendency.

These two questions are key because most investors will not invest in your project unless you have a television broadcast license. They will want to know if there will be a guaranteed audience for the program so that the audience will see the investor's name or company logo in the credits.

Basically, investors want publicity in exchange for their investment. Of course, some investors would like a return on their investment as well.

The Broadcast License

Getting a broadcaster to air your program is critical. The broadcast license will help trigger other funds. There are many television broadcasters in Canada and around the world. You will have to narrow down the list by deciding which broadcasters the program or series would appeal to. Ask yourself: "Is this an idea that would appeal to conventional broadcasters or specialty channels?" In other words, is it a specialized topic that would appeal to a limited audience, or is your idea on a general topic that would attract a wide audience? If your idea is on a specialized topic, do some research and send your idea to broadcasters who air programs similar to yours. These will most likely be specialty cable channels. For example, if your idea is on the hibernation of bears, you will want to send your idea to the Discovery Channel and others that air nature programs.

Getting On the Air

Even if your idea is more general in nature, such as crime in Canada, and several conventional broadcasters might be interested in it, you should still do some research on the broadcasters. You want to make sure that the broadcasters to whom you are sending your idea will air your type of program. Never send your idea to just

Checking the Market

any broadcaster—you will be wasting your time. Always survey the marketplace, in this case the broadcasters, before you develop any proposal as you want to be certain that there will be a market for your idea.

When I was analyzing proposals for broadcasters, I found that ninety percent of all proposals received had nothing to do with the type of programming the broadcasters aired. If only the producers had taken some time to find out what sorts of programs the broadcasters aired, they could have spared themselves time and the disappointment of a rejection letter.

Focus
On the Best Match

First focus on the Canadian broadcasters who would be the best match for your program or series. It is very difficult to sell program ideas to American and foreign broadcasters if you are a new producer. Watch their channels to see what type of programs they air. You can also consult your TV guide which will give you a rundown of all the programs a particular broadcaster will be airing for the week. Or you could call the broadcaster to request a copy of their mission statement; most broadcasters have some type of brochure that describes who they are and what sort of programming they air.

Research Tools

Many broadcasters also distribute their own TV guide which lists their programming on a daily basis. The guide also contains information about individual programs and highlights current and upcoming 'hot' shows. Reading this guide is a good way to get a feel for what the broadcaster is airing. Most of the time you can get the broadcaster to send you their TV guides for free on a bi-monthly or quarterly basis. In some instances you may have to pay a small fee to be placed on their mailing list. If you have an internet connection, check out the broadcaster's website as they usually display their programming schedule on it along with descriptions of individual programs. Sometimes the website will contain guidelines for producers who are interested in sending in program ideas and will give you instructions on what material to send in and to whom.

Another excellent way to find information is to talk to the broadcaster's audience relations department. Most broadcasters have someone who deals with the public and I strongly suggest you utilize these people. They can often give you the information you are looking for and are sometimes a good information resource when you are trying to get through to someone at the broadcaster's who is not returning your phone calls. This is a nasty drawback to working in the entertainment industry. The people who are making decisions are often difficult to get on the phone and more often than not don't return your phone calls. Don't get me wrong, there are many professional people in the industry who do return producers' calls but be forewarned—you will be talking to a lot of voice mail machines in the future.

Utilizing Broadcaster's Relations Department

Ideally, you want your concept to appeal to as many broadcasters as possible so that you can

Generic Ideas

sell it several times. You must be careful, though, not to water down your idea or attempt to make it generic, because then it will appeal to no one. Generic ideas are never well received because there is no real 'meat' to them. By trying to please and interest everybody, they end up satisfying nobody. As well, generic ideas have all been done a thousand times before, while broadcasters want something new or different.

All this brings us to the next stage in analyzing your idea: is it new or different?

Originality

The average broadcaster receives hundreds of proposals for television programs and series every week, so yours has to stand out from the crowd.

What's Your Angle?

If your program is about crime in Canada, what's your angle? There are many programs dealing with crime in Canada, so how is yours different? Do you have a new perspective because you've found experts who believe that the penal system should be thrown out in favour of boot camps? Or have you found a good case study in a former criminal who has an astonishing rehabilitation story? There can be many variations on a story but the trick is to find the angle that hasn't been covered.

Be Realistic

Again, you must be realistic about criticizing your idea. You need money to produce the program and you have to determine whether anyone will invest in it. One sure-fire sign that your idea is not new or different is being turned down cold by every broadcaster that you approach. If this happens to you, move on to a different idea or rethink your current one. Above all else, don't get discouraged.   There may come a time in the future when your project will sell. There will continue to be new broadcasters licensed in Canada and one of them might be interested in your idea. Or there may be a time when your idea just happens to be the hot topic of the moment and you can resubmit your proposal. You may have to leave the proposal on the shelf for awhile. Think of it as future inventory.

The Budget

If you have determined that your idea is original and that no one else has done the story quite like you will do it, your next step is to establish how much it will cost. With the current environment of fiscal restraint, investors want to make sure the budget is not any higher than absolutely necessary.

Determining Your Budget

Be careful though, don't sell your project short. Make sure the budget is realistic. Investors do not want to risk money on a project that might not be completed or that is completed and does not look professional due to lack of funds.

Analyze your idea to make sure funding for the budget would be possible to raise. You don't

Funding A Series

want this to be an overly ambitious project that will never materialize. Many new producers have funding problems when they decide to do a series. I often dealt with new producers who had proposals for a series but found it impossible to raise the money for the entire series. They were eventually able to find enough money to produce one program in the series and had to leave it at that. You should only attempt a series once you have many programs to your credit.

Experienced Producer

Experienced producers have a good idea of how much a project will cost, and don't have to be as concerned about keeping costs low as new producers do. When you have a track record as a producer, investors will not be quite so hesitant about putting money into your projects.

New Producer

If you are a new producer, you should make your budget as low as possible since investors are hesitant to invest their money with new producers. The lower the budget, the lower the risk assumed by an investor. There is, however, a drawback to this low-budget formula. If the budget is too low, the broadcaster will assume that the production will look cheap or be low-quality. Be careful not to skimp on those areas that might affect how the production looks or sounds. To determine the proper budget level, check out the budgets of other productions similar to yours. Or better yet, ask the broadcaster what budget range they prefer to deal with.

Balancing the Budget

On your first project, don't pick an idea that involves a lot of travel. Travel is something that can make a budget skyrocket very quickly. Also, be careful with dramas that involve many actors and many sets; they are very expensive. If you are a new producer, it would be best to begin with a documentary or a short drama as they are the most inexpensive projects to make. Try other genres later as you acquire more experience.

It would also be wise for you to construct the program as a half-hour or hour-long program because other lengths are very difficult to sell to television broadcasters—most of which schedule half-hour and one-hour programs.

The Focus

Your idea must be tightly focussed on one clearly defined subject or no one will be interested in funding it. An idea that is too generic or all over the map ends up confusing the audience as well as making it impossible for you to find funding. It is fine to explore different avenues of the topic or scenario but you must make sure that whatever path you follow, you always end up back at the main storyline.

Finding the Focus

One trick to finding the focus of your story is to write down what the program or series is about in one short paragraph. This written paragraph will be the basis for everything you do on the project. It is the central focus or main idea of your production. Think of it as your mission statement. This paragraph also comes in handy when you write the program or series proposal. It is the first page in your proposal and it helps you to clearly state what you intend to do with the project. If you can't write this paragraph,

Mission Statement

then you have a focus problem, and you must work on finding out what the story is really about before you can proceed any further.

Using crime in Canada as an example, here is a sample focus statement:

Crime in Canada is skyrocketing. This one-hour documentary will focus on where experts say crime begins—in the home. The documentary will follow two families, each with a child in a juvenile detention centre, to determine if the children's home life was a contributing factor to their crimes.

Checklist

Analyzing Your Idea

Once you have analyzed your idea using all of the suggestions in this chapter, you will be ready to begin writing the program proposal. The proposal is the most important selling tool for your project. Just remember to answer the following questions to analyze your idea.

1. Is the idea new or different?
2. Will the idea appeal to broadcasters? Which broadcasters?
3. How much will the project cost?
4. Can this idea be realistically accomplished financially as well as creatively?
5. What is the project's focus?

Chapter Two

Drawing the Blueprint—The Television Proposal

The program or series proposal is the one document that will trigger production financing. It explains what the project is about, how it will look, and how much it will cost. The proposal is critical because investors use it to determine how well the idea will translate to the screen. They will also use it to determine if the producer can complete the project and how good the production will look. The proposal is basically the producer's most important calling card. Generally, the proposal only needs to be about ten pages in length. A few funding bodies request that a proposal be longer in order to include market studies and promotional plans, but this is unusual.

The Producer's Calling Card

In order to be certain of what to include in the proposal, it's best to check with the investor or broadcaster in advance. Most broadcasters and investors are so well organized that they can make available to you official guidelines for submitting proposals. If the funding source offers no guidelines, write only what is needed in the proposal (see the checklist at the end of this chapter). Don't give an overly detailed background on the subject or include unnecessary information.

Remember, those who make the decisions about which projects to fund read hundreds of

Overkill Proposals

proposals every month, so don't annoy them with excess or useless paperwork. When I was analyzing program proposals for broadcasters, I found that many proposals contained pages and pages of unnecessary background information. The real proposal could have been written in just two or three pages. These overkill proposals generally came from inexperienced producers who felt that the more information they added, the more credible their proposal would be. As a guideline for writing your proposal, a sample proposal is included at the end of this chapter.

Presentation

A Professional Proposal

Because you are seeking funding in a highly competitive environment, it is important that the proposal look as professional as possible. You can print the proposal on regular white paper or buy a thicker stock of lightly coloured paper. Use 8-1/2 by 11 paper and type the proposal single-spaced on a computer.

Always remember to spell-check the proposal once you have finished with it; spelling mistakes indicate that you are not paying attention to quality, which may concern potential investors. I once worked with a Programming Director who would circle all of the spelling mistakes in a producer's proposal while reading it.

The Binding

Professional Appearance

In order to make your proposal look as professional as possible, get it bound in an attractive manner. Do not just staple it together. Go down to your local print shop and get it cerloxed, spiral bound or place it in an attractive binder. Spend a bit of money to make it look professional. Some investors such as government funding bodies specify in their guidelines that they do not want proposals to be bound as they need to make photocopies. In this case, you can use a clear report cover that acts as the front and back cover and is closed with a plastic slide-on clip to make dismantling easier.

The Title Page

The title page of the proposal should contain the name of the program or series in bold letters, centred at the top of the page. If you can find a colour photograph or drawing that depicts what your proposal is about, place it under the main title. Colour photographs are great because they add life to the page and help to distinguish your proposal from many others. Do not include an actual photograph on the title page, use a colour photocopy. As well, make sure that the photo is fairly professional looking—home snapshots will not do. Pictures from magazines also make good cover images; they give the reader a feel for the project.

Distinguish Your Proposal

If you can't find a photo you like, place a computer graphic on the page or simply choose a font that makes the page look more attractive. At the bottom of the title page, type your name or company name followed by your address and phone number. Your name and address must be evident on the proposal in case the cover letter you will be sending with the proposal gets separated from the package.

Perception
Is Everything

Making the cover of this proposal attractive and professional looking is very important. You would be surprised if you knew how much further your proposal will get if the outside packaging looks attractive. The person reading the proposal will be more impressed and may look more favourably upon the program idea. This may seem simplistic, but it really works. When I was faced with reading many proposals a day and would look at the endless stack on my desk, the ones that looked more attractive stood out and seemed more credible. Therefore, the second golden rule of producing is 'perception is everything.' If you and your proposal look successful, you will be perceived as being successful. You must remember that in the entertainment business, products and programs that look glitzy and snazzy on the outside are more attractive to people. For example, how many times have you seen a trailer for a movie that made the film look sensational but when you went to see the movie all of the best moments had been shown in the trailer? You must apply this same technique to the cover of your proposal and place a lot of effort into making the cover of the proposal look sensational.

Copyright Concerns

At the bottom of the title page, type 'copyright,' followed by the year and your name or your company's name. This lets the reader know that the material is copyrighted and cannot be appropriated.   Most people are under the impression that you have to register your idea for copyright to exist, but this is not the case. Copyright exists as soon as the idea is placed in a tangible form such as the written word.

New producers tend to be concerned about sending their idea to broadcasters for fear of having the broadcaster steal the idea.   This seems to be an ungrounded fear; I have not yet heard of a case in Canada where a producer had his or her idea stolen by a broadcaster. You do hear of this happening in the United States, primarily in the feature film business, but Canadian broadcasters usually operate with a great deal of professionalism and high ethical standards, so this is not a cause for much concern.

The Project Focus

The first page of the proposal should be what I call the project focus. You can take the project description paragraph you wrote in chapter one and place it at the centre of a new page with the program or series title at the top.   This will provide a quick description of your proposal for the busy reader. This paragraph may come in very handy later, so make it sound as attractive as possible. Write it as if it is a description that will appear in a TV guide.

An Attractive Proposal

For example, if you were looking over what was on TV one night and came across a very interesting description of a program in the TV guide, you would be interested in watching it. You want to do the same thing with your project focus. Write it in such a way that the person who is reading your proposal feels interested enough to continue reading on. It's often reported that Hollywood investors want to know what your idea is about in one sentence, so make the most out of your one paragraph. You may consider placing another photo or image on this page; the more images and colour you add to the rest of your proposal, the more you will enhance the proposal's presentation value.

The Story Synopsis

Present It Well
On Paper

The next step in the proposal is a story synopsis, in other words an expanded description of what the program or series is about. The synopsis is the lengthiest section of the proposal, but should never run longer than five pages. I have seen some very good story ideas synopsized in a single page. The trick is to be clear and concise. Don't clutter your synopsis with unnecessary information.

Your proposal will be one of many proposals the prospective investors will be reading, so you want to capture their attention immediately. If you can't get their attention, you risk having them lose interest in your project. The general rule is: "If you can't present your idea well on paper, how are you going to translate that idea to the screen?"

The Story Treatment

The story treatment follows the synopsis. It is a one- to two-page description of the style and tone of the production. Basically, it explains how the program or series will look on-screen. Some investors don't require a story treatment, but even if it isn't a prerequisite, it's best to include the treatment as it helps the investor to visualize how the production will look. Remember, not all investors are familiar with television production.

A Creative Look At Production

The treatment is usually considered to be the director's vision of how the production is going to be filmed. You don't actually have to have a director write the treatment; you can act as the director and describe what sort of look you are going to achieve. For example, are you going to shoot it in black and white for a cinema vérité style or are you going to shoot it with a Betacam camera to achieve a documentary feel?

Director's Vision

You should also write about how the story is going to unfold. Will there be an on-air host, voice-over narration or is it a drama in which the characters will speak for themselves?

Mention the sort of music or lighting you will be using. Basically, you want to explain what sort of mood you will convey during the production. Be creative in this area of the proposal because the creative look of the production is what the treatment is all about.

Mood of the Production

The Budget

Long- and Short-Form Budgets

The budget details how much the production will cost and how the money will be spent. The budget can be written in two ways: the long-form budget following the Telefilm Canada format, named after one of Canada's leading funders, or the short-form budget which is called the top sheet. The long-form budget is very detailed and several pages in length. It requires you to present every expenditure you anticipate making during production.

Top Sheet—Five Main Categories

The top sheet usually runs one page in length and contains all the same information as the long-form budget, but without the detailed item breakdowns. It includes the following five main categories of expenditure:

a) *Above-the-Line Costs*—These are fixed costs, costs that will remain the same. They cannot cause the production to go over budget. Costs in this category include the producer's and director's fees and any development costs.

b) *Below-the-Line Costs*—These costs are related to the production of the program and represent what you see on the screen. These are non-fixed costs which means they can cause the production to go over budget. Costs in this category include crew and equipment fees, travel, etc.

c) *Post-Production Costs*—These costs are related to the editing and assembly of the raw footage. Costs in this category include editorial labour, equipment and music rights.

d) *Indirect Costs*—These are costs that are not directly related to the production of the program. They include publicity, insurance and general office expenses.

e) *Contingency*—Contingency is extra money put aside for cost overruns; sort of a rainy-day savings. The contingency can be anywhere from five to fifteen percent of the entire budget, excluding above-the-line and indirect costs.

Some investors, such as public and private funding agencies, require you to submit a long-form budget while other investors, such as broadcasters, require only the top sheet. It's best to ask the investor how detailed a budget to include. When in doubt, send both a long-form budget and the top sheet.

Calculating the Budget

Calculating the budget might seem like a daunting task to a new producer, but it doesn't need to be. Assess how many days of filming and how many crew members you will need, calculate crew fees based on their daily rate, and then come up with a realistic budget. If you are unsure of what amounts to put in, call local service providers, such as equipment-rental houses or post-production facilities, and ask for their rates. This will give you a good idea of the value of the services and equipment.

Experienced producers can complete a budget very quickly. They have gone through this procedure before and know how much money it will take to complete a project. Generally, experienced producers take the budget from their previous project and increase it slightly for their current project. With each new project, the producer gains more experience and is more interested in placing a larger sum of money in the current project.

Budget Template

You can either make a budget template yourself following the Telefilm format or buy a computer program that contains a budget on disk. You can also find books about television and film budgets in larger bookstores that explain the budgeting process and contain budget templates.

A word of advice for both new and experienced producers: always double-check your budget for any mathematical errors. It is very easy for errors to slip past as the budget is often revised several times. When I was reviewing producers' proposals, I often found errors in the budgets.

If a budget error is discovered after contracts for funds have been drafted, you will have to go through lengthy processes to get the contracts corrected. So no matter how many times you have checked your budget, check it again!

The Finance Plan

Where 'The Buck Starts'

The finance plan is a list of all the organizations you hope to receive funding from, and it details the amounts of money you may have already received. The finance plan mirrors the total amount of your budget. For example, if your budget is $150,000, you have to show on the finance plan where you are going to get the $150,000.

If you have some funding already in place, list these amounts along with the names of the organizations that gave you the money. These are called confirmed sources of financing. Confirmed sources are listed on the finance plan along with unconfirmed sources of financing. Your list of unconfirmed sources should include amounts that you hope to receive and the names of the organizations from which you hope to receive them.

Sources of Funding

To signify to the investor that the amounts are unconfirmed, write 'unconfirmed' or 'antici-pated' next to the amount. You must be able to prove you have done some research on these unconfirmed amounts. You cannot simply list any figure you hope to receive. Contact funding organizations to determine how much money they would invest should your proposal be accepted. Some organizations include the approximate amounts they give in their proposal guidelines. Others, like broadcasters, have a set range that they pay and will readily give you this information. Use their mid-range figure in your finance plan.

'Anticipated'
or
'Unconfirmed'
Payments

There will usually be a portion of the finance plan that you won't be able to account for no matter how hard you fundraise. You can cover this missing amount by listing it as a deferral or

Deferred Payments

producer's investment. Deferral is a situation whereby one or more of the key production team won't take a salary up front and will only get paid once the project is fully funded. It's usually the producer's salary that is listed as a deferred payment because the producer's job is to make sure that everyone else gets paid first.

The Production Schedule

Production Schedule: Four Key Areas

The production schedule, which follows the finance plan, is a one-page estimate of the dates when each phase of the production process begins. Investors need to know approximately what date the production will be completed. Investors need this information in order to determine what budget year the funding should be drawn on and if the delivery date will mesh with the time in which they need the production to be aired. Investors know that the production schedule is just an estimate on your part so you will not need to keep to the exact schedule. Nevertheless, your estimate should be realistic.

In the production schedule you need to deal with four key areas: pre-production, production, post-production, and the delivery date for the completed project. You don't have to list the exact day you anticipate you will be completing each stage. Simply list the appropriate month. For example:

a) Pre-Production: January - February
b) Production: March

c) Post-Production: April - July
d) Delivery: August 1st

Draft Script

If your production is a drama or comedy, and thus requires scripts, you need to include a draft scene in the proposal. Make sure there is a paragraph or two to introduce the scene so the reader evaluating your proposal understands the context and action. Choose a short scene for inclusion because the reader's time is limited.

Draft Scene

The Producer's Resume

An important item in the proposal is the producer's resume. Ultimately, whether your project gets funded or not will probably depend on your level of ability. Funding agencies and broadcasters are going to look very closely at your past experience. This, of course, is an area where new producers will be at a disadvantage. It is an unfortunate truth that in the television industry a lack of experience is the second-largest deterrent for new producers, next to not having connections.

Producer's Level of Ability

If you are a new producer, list all the experience you have had on other productions such as being a crew member or working on student productions (although don't make a point of calling them student productions). Make your experience relevant to the task at hand.

Make Your Experience Relevant

Sometimes new producers come from fields other than the entertainment industry because they have a particular area of expertise that compels them to produce a specific project. If this is your case, then state what your particular area of expertise is and how this is beneficial or necessary for the project. For example, if the program is about the hibernation of bears and you are an animal behavior specialist, then stress how your specialized training will allow you to capture the essence of the project in a way that no other producer can. This might help to strengthen your case by proving that while you do not have experience as a producer, you do have intimate knowledge of the subject.

Team Work

The best advice to any new producer is to team up with an experienced producer, either working as a partner or hired as a co-producer or executive producer. You will benefit from this person's track record and experience in part because it will make investors less reluctant to invest in a new and unknown producer. Be cautious when the experienced producer wants you to sign over all rights in the production to them. Make sure you get a fair deal.

Team Resume

If you are working with an experienced producer, director, cameraperson or actor, include their resumes in your proposal as well. This will give the investor more faith in your production team's abilities. If you need to include more than three resumes, write a summary paragraph on each person's ability instead of a long resume and only include an expanded resume for yourself. Your resume should be no longer than three pages in length and should list only your relevant production experience. It is not the standard resume you would submit while job hunting.

If you have produced before, list the names of the productions and the years in which they were produced along with the names of the broadcasters who aired them. It's helpful to submit one VHS tape of a sample of your previous work.

Letters of Support

If you have already attracted a broadcaster or other funding bodies to your project, include letters of support from these institutions. This will show people who are reading your proposal that you already have some funding in place. If you can think of any other organization or person who might lend credibility to your proposal by writing a letter, include it in the proposal as well. For example, if you were producing the "Crime in Canada" documentary you might want to approach government bodies, interested citizen groups, and non-profit organizations who would write you a letter of support.

Using the three-page rule, only send a maximum of three letters of support. Don't stuff your proposal full of letters to annoy the reader. I once had a situation where a producer wanted to fax some letters of support for a proposal they had submitted. 'Some' turned out to be about

Three-Page Rule

twenty, which was annoying enough because this tied up the fax machine, but when the producer mistakenly thought the fax did not go through, all the letters were sent through again. What a horror!

Promo Tape

Sample Footage to Further Your Case

If you have the money and the time, include a VHS-format, short promotional tape of some of the scenes of your production. To make the tape, shoot some sample footage. In the case of a documentary, you could perhaps film interviews with key people who will be appearing in the documentary and for dramas or comedies, film a brief scene with your actors and put the footage together with some basic editing. Clearly mark the tape as a promo tape and explain in your cover letter that this is sample footage you have assembled to give the reader a visual idea of the nature of the production.

I have seen promo tapes successfully change the mind of investors who were not going to invest in a project because they felt the producer did not have enough experience. If you do include a promo tape, it is very important that it is professionally produced and shot, and that the audio is audible. Obviously, you should never include a promo tape that is substandard or resembles the quality of a home video. Include only footage that furthers your case that this production is a worthwhile investment.

Demo Tape

If you have produced before , including high-quality student productions, include a VHS sample of your work. Again, clearly mark this as a demo tape of your work. You can also include a sample of your director's or camera-person's previous work if you don't have a tape of your own work to submit. Don't submit too many VHS tapes; one is the best to send but if you feel that submitting an extra tape would lend credibility to your proposal, then send it in. Just realize that you probably won't get the tapes back so never send your only copy.

Lend Credibility to Your Proposal

The Cover Letter

Once the proposal is completed, you need to write a personalized cover letter to each potential investor. In the letter, you want to state that you are including a proposal, the subject of your proposal, and that you are seeking investment for the production. If you have already lined up investors or, specifically, a broadcast license, state this in the letter. Investors like to know that there will be an audience for the production and that there are other investors.

Personalized Cover Letter

A Word to the Wise

Now that you know all the steps to writing a proposal, it's important to get your idea down on paper as soon as possible. Don't spend excess time rewriting the proposal or researching facets of your idea. It's certainly imperative that you

Get Your Idea Down On Paper

are very knowledgeable about your idea and that you have clearly thought out what your program or series is about and exactly how you are going to make it a reality. What I mean is don't spend a year or more researching and writing as you have no guarantee that your idea will be accepted.

This is the reality of the business. There is only a finite amount of money and few television slots available. With many producers vying for the same opportunities, it's inevitable that a lot of ideas are going to be rejected. Proposals for television programming are a case in which there is more supply than demand. There are more producers trying to pitch ideas to television stations than there are stations willing to pay for them. Be prudent and do your homework. Write a clear, concise, easily understood proposal but don't spend many months doing it as you could be using this time to think up other marketable ideas.

Be Simple and Matter-of-Fact

I often believe that doing a lot of research is a form of procrastination. The research phase keeps you away from writing the proposal. Don't make writing the proposal into a difficult task. Think of it as if you were explaining your concept to a friend. You would explain it in a simple, matter-of-fact way. There is an old saying with the acronym KISS which stands for 'keep it simple stupid.' This is how the proposal should be written. You want to provide enough facts that the person reading it will understand immediately what your idea is about, but not so many facts that it appears as if you are writing a dissertation.

Many of the proposals I have read were so confusing that by the last page of the proposal, I still didn't have any idea what the program was about. Don't let this happen to you.

Success Stories

Now that you know how to write a proposal, you can be a little creative in getting it approved. Some producers think up very creative ways to get their proposals noticed. One enterprising producer who had an idea for a documentary that included a stand-up comedy component arranged a meeting with an investor and brought a stand-up comedian to the meeting. The comedian did a five-minute routine and, based on its success, the producer found a new investor. Another success story involved producers who had an idea for a series about stockbrokers. They picked up the potential investor in a limousine, held the meeting at a stock exchange and successfully negotiated the deal.

Creativity Kicks In

In order to make your proposal a success, you don't necessarily have to think up gimmicks. All you need is a solidly written and professionally presented proposal. You, as producer, are only limited by your imagination and your ability to succeed. If you are determined that the project will succeed, then it probably will with a great deal of patience and persistence on your part. It may mean making some revisions to your proposal or going back to the drawing

Patience and Persistence

board, but if you have the enthusiasm and the determination, your production will become a reality.

Checklist

To recap, here are all of the components of a good proposal and the order in which they should appear.

1. Cover Letter
2. Title Page
3. Project Focus
4. Story Synopsis
5. Story Treatment
6. Budget
7. Finance Plan
8. Production Schedule
9. Draft Script (if applicable)
10. Resumes
11. Letters of Support
12. Promo Tape or Demo Tape

Sample Proposal Cover Letter

Date:

Jane Black
DEF Television Broadcasting
Toronto, ON
M1B 2C3

Dear Ms. Black:

I am sending you a proposal for an hour-long documentary on a man named John Smith, which I believe would make a fascinating addition to your *Canadian Justice* television series. I have tentatively entitled the documentary "Breakout: the John Smith Story."

John Smith has been in the Canadian news regularly since the 1960's. In 1968, Smith was sentenced to life in prison for the shooting death of a variety store attendant. Smith has always claimed that he is innocent of the murder and has gone to great lengths to prove it.

Over the years, Smith has steadfastly tried to get someone— including the Attorney General, the press and the murdered man's family—to look into his case. In 1990 he broke out of prison, finally drawing to his case the attention he craved. An intensive manhunt was conducted and through a bizarre twist of events, Smith was arrested on his way down to meet with his lawyer, where he had planned to turn himself in. The justice committee has agreed to look into Smith's case, but he is now in a maximum-security prison with no hope of parole.

This, of course, is a capsulized version of John Smith's fascinating story. The documentary will fully explore Smith's arrest and claims of innocence.

I have several sources of funding already confirmed for the documentary, as detailed in the finance plan. I am now looking for a national broadcaster for the project. I am confident that this documentary will make an interesting addition to the *Canadian Justice* series. I look forward to hearing from you soon.

Yours truly,

Jill Brown

Sample Proposal Title Page

BREAKOUT: THE JOHN SMITH STORY

[PHOTO]

Produced By:

Jill Brown
A1 Productions
123 Hope Street
Montreal, Quebec
M4E 5F6

copyright © (year)

Sample Proposal Project Focus

BREAKOUT: THE JOHN SMITH STORY

Breakout: The John Smith Story, is a 60-minute documentary about the arrest, conviction, and jail-break of Canadian fugitive John Smith. The documentary will explore Smith's claims that he was wrongly convicted and his attempts to clear his name by breaking out of prison. Suspenseful and thought-provoking, this documentary will lead viewers to question whether Smith is guilty or is an innocent man wasting away in prison.

[PHOTO]

Sample Proposal Story Synopsis

Breakout: The John Smith Story is a 60-minute documentary on the arrest, conviction, and jail-break of fugitive John Smith.

John Smith is a 65-year-old inmate of Orillia Penitentiary. He has been in prison for twenty long, meaningless years. He has a long time yet to go as he is serving a life term for second-degree murder, a crime which he claims he did not commit.

Life has never been kind to Smith, who has lived only twenty-two years of his life outside of jail. Fate dealt him a blow early in life when he was placed in a boys' home when his mother could no longer take care of him because of his alcoholic father. Smith never saw his father again, but his mother often came to visit him at the home. She always had a smile but despite her constant assurances that she would take him out of the home, it never came to pass as his mother never escaped her own private torture. She was brutally beaten to death one night by her husband.

Smith lived the rest of his teenage years in the boys' home, a cruel, merciless place where physical punishment was often meted out. Smith fell in with a group of older boys and together they would shoplift from stores as a way to get nice clothing and possessions. The shoplifting eventually turned to petty thievery, and Smith was caught one day while breaking into a house. As he was now old enough to be criminally charged, the judge sent him to a juvenile detention centre where he was to begin his first sentence for a crime. This sentence was followed by others, for as soon as Smith was released from the centre he would commit more crimes for which he was inevitably caught. And so began the cycle which most criminals are unable to break: the cycle of going to jail, getting out and committing more crimes.

In 1978 Smith was released and began a robbery spree with one of his old cellmates, David Green. In late January they robbed a house and used the money to buy drugs. High on drugs and feeling fine, the two men pulled into an 24-hour variety store. Green said he would go in to buy cigarettes while Smith should wait in the car. Time stretched on and Smith dozed while waiting for Green to return. Green did return with an armful of cash and told Smith to "Get out of there quick." Green had noticed that the cash register was full and had pulled out a gun demanding money from the young clerk. When the clerk refused, Green calmly shot him in the head and fled with the money. Now Smith was tied up in something more serious than robbery and realized he had to get out of the country. While trying to cross the border into the United States, he was captured and sent to jail to await trial for his crimes.

Smith was found guilty of second-degree murder and even though he did not commit the crime, was given a life sentence. Smith has always maintained his innocence, filing numerous appeals and writing to anyone who may help his cause. He turned his life around while in prison, married Kate, a long-time supporter of his innocence and began reading law books to help his case. Then one day a ladder was left by some workmen who were installing new lights around the prison, and Smith used it to climb over the high prison wall into freedom.

Smith survived by living in an abandoned barn and eating garbage. He lived this way for two weeks before breaking into a farmhouse to call his lawyer. A meeting was arranged the next day and while Smith was making his way downtown, he was spotted by a policeman and taken back into custody. This is where Smith sits today, in prison for a crime he says he didn't commit. But the evidence points to Smith as one of the murderers. All sides to this fascinating story will be explored but in the end the audience will be left to decide; is he innocent or guilty of the murder?

Sample Proposal Story Treatment

The focus of **Breakout: The John Smith Story** is the question of John Smith's guilt. Several people knowledgeable about the case will be interviewed, some who believe Smith is innocent, others who believe he is guilty. The documentary will be balanced so that viewers can draw their own conclusions about Smith's guilt or innocence.

The documentary will begin with the arrest of the two men on the charge of murder. News footage of the murder scene and prison photos of the men will be used. Interviews will be conducted with the detective in charge of the investigation and with the victim's family. The evidence against the two men will be featured.

Next the documentary will focus on Smith's life before the murder. His childhood will be explored as well as his life before prison. Interviews with Smith's wife will be conducted.

After covering Smith's background, the documentary will move to the conviction of Smith and Green. This will be the first time in the documentary that Smith will be heard from. Smith will explain why he was arrested and why he is innocent of the crime. Green will also be interviewed to explain how he alone murdered the variety-store clerk.

The documentary will then move to Smith's breakout from prison. Smith eluded capture by hiding in an abandoned barn. During this time Smith's wife Kate pleaded with him via the media to turn himself in. News footage of the manhunt for Smith will be used along with footage of Kate Smith's pleas to her husband. Interviews with several subjects, including Smith's lawyer, family, the police captain in charge of the manhunt, and the victim's family will be filmed.

After two weeks of hiding from the police, Smith was captured while making his way downtown to a meeting with his lawyer.

The documentary will end with John Smith back in prison. Members of the audience will be left to decide for themselves whether he is innocent or guilty of the murder.

There will be no host for the documentary and little narration. The only narration will be at the beginning (to establish the story) and at the end (to draw the story to a conclusion). This method will allow the interviewees to tell their own stories in their own words.

The lighting will be dark and somber throughout the documentary and the camera will be on medium to tight closeups of the interviewees. There will be little music and few graphics. The intent is to show the audience John Smith's growing desperation.

Top-Sheet (Short-Form) Budget

ACCOUNT NUMBER	ACCOUNT DESCRIPTION	RATE $	PERIOD	TOTAL $
02	Scenario			3,500
03	Development Costs			2,500
04	Producer			10,000
05	Director			6,000
	ABOVE-THE-LINE TOTAL — A			$ 22,000
10	Cast			1,300
12	Production Staff			4,125
22	Camera Labour			7,125
25	Sound Labour			5,625
28	Production Office Expenses			6,000
32	Unit Expenses			5,000
33	Travel & Living Expenses			6,700
45	Camera Equipment			6,750
46	Electrical Equipment			2,250
48	Sound Equipment			1,500
50	Tape Stock			1,400
51	Production Laboratory			2,225
	PRODUCTION TOTAL — B			$ 50,000
60	Editorial Labour			13,500
61	Editorial Equipment			11,250
62	Post Production (Picture)			6,000
63	Post Production (Sound)			3,000
66	Music			6,000
67	Titles/Stock Footage			8,500
68	Versioning			1,750
	POST PRODUCTION TOTAL — C			$ 50,000
70	Unit Publicity			2,500
71	General Expenses/Overhead			7,000
72	Indirect Costs			5,000
	OTHER CHARGES — D			$ 14,500
80	Contingency (B+Cx10%)			10,000
GRAND TOTAL				$ 146,500

Long Form Budget

ACCOUNT NUMBER	ACCOUNT DESCRIPTION	RATE $	PERIOD	TOTAL $
ABOVE-THE-LINE				
01	Story Rights/Acquisition			
02	Scenario			3,500
03	Development Costs			2,500
04	Producer			10,000
05	Director			6,000
06	Stars			
ABOVE-THE-LINE TOTAL — A				$ 22,000
BELOW-THE-LINE — PRODUCTION				
10	Cast	650	2 days	1,300
11	Extras			
12	Production Staff	275	15 days	4,125
13	Design Labour			
14	Construction Labour			
15	Set Dressing Labour			
16	Props Labour			
17	Special Effects Labour			
18	Wrangling Labour			
19	Wardrobe Labour			
20	Makeup/Hair Labour			
21	Video Technical Crew			
22	Camera Labour	475	15 days	7,125
23	Electrical Labour			
24	Grip Labour			
25	Sound Labour	375	15 days	5,625
26	Transportation Labour			
27	Fringe Benefits			
28	Production Office Expenses	allow		6,000
29	Studio/Backlot Expenses			
30	Location Office Expenses			
31	Site Expenses			
32	Unit Expenses	allow		5,000

ACCOUNT NUMBER	ACCOUNT DESCRIPTION	RATE $	PERIOD	TOTAL $
33	Travel & Living Expenses	allow		6,700
34	Transportation			
35	Construction Materials			
36	Art Supplies			
37	Set Dressing			
38	Props			
39	Special Effects			
40	Animals			
41	Wardrobe Supplies			
42	Makeup/Hair Supplies			
43	Video Studio Facilities			
44	Video Remote Tech Facilities			
45	Camera Equipment	450	15 days	6,750
46	Electrical Equipment	150	15 days	2,250
47	Grip Equipment			
48	Sound Equipment	100	15 days	1,500
49	Second Unit			
50	Tape Stock	35	40 tapes	1,400
51	Production Laboratory	allow		2,225
PRODUCTION TOTAL — B				**$ 50,000**
BELOW-THE-LINE — POST-PRODUCTION				
60	Editorial Labour	300	45 days	13,500
61	Editorial Equipment	250	45 days	11,250
62	Post Production (Picture)	2,000	3 days	6,000
63	Post Production (Sound)	600	5 days	3,000
64	Post Production Office			
65	Film Post Production Sound			
66	Music	allow		6,000
67	Titles/Stock Footage	allow		8,500
68	Versioning	allow		1,750
69	Amortizations (Series)			
POST PRODUCTION TOTAL — C				**$ 50,000**

ACCOUNT NUMBER	ACCOUNT DESCRIPTION	RATE $	PERIOD	TOTAL $
BELOW-THE-LINE — OTHER CHARGES				
70	Unit Publicity	allow		2,500
71	General Expenses	allow		7,000
72	Indirect Costs/Overhead	allow		5,000
OTHER CHARGES TOTAL — D				$ 14,500
TOTAL A+B+C+D				$ 136,500
80	Contingency (B + C x 10%)			10,000
81	Completion Guarantee			
82	Cost of Issue			
GRAND TOTAL				$ 146,500

Finance Plan

Canadian Broadcaster—national window	$	35,000
Television Fund (ANTICIPATED)	$	22,000
Tax Credits	$	20,550
Grant from the Ministry of Justice	$	15,000
Documentary Fund	$	14,950
Producer Deferral (AS MORE FUNDS COME IN, THIS FIGURE WILL BE REDUCED)	$	10,000
Foundations (ANTICIPATED)	$	10,000
Canadian Broadcasters—provincial windows	$	8,000
Director Deferral	$	6,000
Private Investors	$	5,000
TOTAL	**$**	**146,500**

Production Schedule

Pre-Production:	January - February
Production:	March
Post-Production:	April - July
Delivery:	August 1st

Resumes

Jill Brown — Producer

Jill Brown has been in the television industry for over 10 years. She successfully moved from being a camera operator in the late '80's to an accomplished television producer today. She has produced numerous television productions such as "How Not to be Canadian," shown on the CBC, "Samurai Warriors," the series for History Television and "Coldfish" for the Discovery Channel.

Maryanne Noire — Director

Maryanne Noire is a director for television as well as film and has directed such notable programs as "Let's Talk About It" from No Communication Productions and "She Likes Chocolate" from Skinny Pictures. Maryanne has also produced and directed her own projects such as "Headhunters" for which she won a Special Mention at the Toronto Film Festival.

Michelle Blanc — Cameraperson

Michelle Blanc has been a cameraperson for five years and has also been director of photography on several films. She began her career as a cameraperson on Best-Dressed Productions "Ragtime Theater" which aired on CTV. She then worked on numerous corporate videos before becoming a cameraperson on the long-running PBS series We Want Your Money. Michelle is the first woman to be awarded the Golden Camera Award from the Production Society of Canada.

Chapter Three

Do the Hustle—Where to Find Financing

Now that you've written your proposal, it's time to send it out. This is almost like planning a military strategy. First let's see how the financing of Canadian television programming works.

The Canadian television industry is experiencing a generally healthy climate but finding financing for television can best be described as putting together a jigsaw puzzle. Producers have to look to many different sources to find production money. It's not simple like the British system. If you're a British producer and are lucky enough to get one of the television networks interested in your production, they will fund almost the entire budget of the project so you don't have to look elsewhere for money. But it's not as hard as the American system, where most of the funding comes from large television networks whose general policy it is to deal only with producers they know, so breaking into the American market is very difficult.

Putting Together the Jigsaw Puzzle

In Canada, we are fortunate to have government programs that provide funding for television programs made by Canadian producers. This doesn't mean you will get the money automatically. Among other criteria, you will have to prove that you have the ability to

Role of the Canadian Government

carry out the project and have stable financing for your project. The Canadian government supports the television industry to a degree where if you're a competent producer, you have a chance at getting government funding. These government funds are triggered by convincing Canadian broadcasters to grant you a broadcast license. Once you have obtained this license, you can apply to various government agencies which will match a percentage of your project's budget.

Finding All of the Pieces of The Pie

After selling the program to broadcasters, and accessing government funds, producers then try a multitude of funding schemes such as accessing grants from government departments, television industry funds, charitable foundations, corporate sponsors, foreign broadcasters, distributors, and the list goes on. The game plan is to find all of the pieces of the pie to make a whole. If we were to dissect this pie crumb by crumb, the sources listed in this chapter would be some of the main components.

National Television Broadcasters

As mentioned previously, the first step in getting your program or series off the ground is to find a television broadcaster who will broadcast your project. Once your proposal is finished, you need to target the broadcasters to whom you are going to send it. You should start with national broadcasters first; these are the Canadian television networks or specialty channels that broadcast across Canada. You begin with them because they generally give

you the largest sum of money for your program. *Your First Window*
The money they give you is in exchange for a *of Opportunity*
national television license to broadcast your program for a certain number of years, and a certain
number of times, coast to coast across Canada.
This is also sometimes called 'first window' as
the broadcaster gets the first window of
opportunity to air your project before any other
television outlet. You will learn that this is the
law of television land; whoever pays the most
goes first.

Targeting these national broadcasters goes
back to chapter one when you did your research
on which broadcasters might be interested in
your project. Once you have found the one or
two national broadcasters who might be
interested in your idea, call them up and ask the
receptionist, audience relations person, or someone in the programming department, to whom
you should send your proposal. As a hint,
always make friends with the secretary or
assistant in the programming department. Like
the audience relations person, the secretary is
always a good source of information.

There is usually someone in the program- *Pitching Your Idea*
ming department whose job it is to deal with
independent producers and their proposals,
they may be called the Director of Programming
or some other similar title. You may want to call
that person directly and ask if you can send
them a proposal, but they are generally very
busy, harried individuals, who are *pitched*
programming ideas day and night by producers
to the point where one Programming Director

told me of once being followed into the bath-room at an industry function and pitched to in front of the stalls by a producer.

Approaching the
Programming Director
The Right Way

Talking to these people is always a good bet so you get an idea what they are looking for, and if your project would interest them. This way you're not wasting your time and theirs by send-ing in a proposal that wouldn't suit them. Be cautious though, these people are often hard to get a hold of and don't like being bombarded by phone calls from producers. If you do get through to them, be short and to-the-point about what your proposal is about and ask if you can send it to them. Above all else, if they say that your project does not fit their agenda, don't argue, instead ring off courteously. It does not help your case to argue because, believe me, they will remember the argument if they talk to you in the future.

Once you have determined to which national broadcasters to send the proposal, and you have reasonably ascertained that they may be interest-ed, send it in. This is always the point where I say a little prayer over the package before drop-ping it in the mail, not because I'm a religious person but because I feel I'll need all the help I can get.

Waiting for A Response

The next thing you will do is what all pro-ducers eventually spend most of their time doing—waiting for a response. You may get a letter back acknowledging receipt of your proposal and stating that you will have to wait six to eight weeks to receive a reply. They may also want you to sign a release form that says you acknowledge that the broadcaster receives programming ideas that may be similar or the same as yours and that you will not sue for copyright infringement. Sign the form and send it back as it is a formality you have to go through before they will read your proposal.

Then you wait for long, agonizing months. I suggest that if you haven't heard from them within one month after their receipt of your proposal, you call the person to whom you sent the proposal, confirm that they received it and explain that you are looking for a response. I believe that you deserve a response. No matter how busy they are, they should take the time to get back to you.

Be forewarned that most of the responses you will get back from broadcasters and other funding bodies will be negative. They will send you nice, polite letters saying that your project is not for them, better luck elsewhere. The first few times this happens it will be hard to take but you will develop a thick skin as more rejections pile up. Rejection is a hard pill to swallow, but unfortunately it is something you will encounter often.

Rejection—A Hard Pill to Swallow

Provincial Broadcasters

After you have sent your proposal to national broadcasters, next on your hit list are Canadian provincial broadcasters. These are television stations in each province that broadcast only within their provincial boundaries. In some cases, their signals reach throughout the province, in other cases their signal is carried only within a geographic area. The stations that broadcast across the entire province will generally be interested in any genre or topic of programming while the stations that air only within a particular area are usually only interested in programming that deals with local topics or issues.

The Second Window   Both of these types of television stations will buy programming from independent producers but buy on a smaller scale and give smaller license fees than national broadcasters. How it works is the national broadcaster airs the program exclusively for a certain period of time after which the provincial broadcasters can air it. This is why the provincial broadcast license is often called the 'second window.'

As with national broadcasters, you should find out who the provincial broadcasters are and what type of programming they buy. One hint is to start with the stations within your own province as some of these broadcasters have a mandate to purchase programs from local producers.

If you are lucky, you might be able to sell to two or three provincial broadcasters. If you are a real salesperson, you might be able to sell to even more. The only drawback to selling your program to provincial broadcasters is that they only give you money for the license fee once the program is completed, which makes it hard when you need money in advance.

Government Funding Agencies

After getting a broadcaster on board, most producers apply to government funding agencies. There are several national as well as provincial government agencies who provide funding for Canadian television, with the largest agency being Telefilm Canada. As a general rule these agencies will only give you funds if you have a broadcast license.

Receiving funds from these agencies is very competitive, with many producers vying for the funds. These funds usually come in the form of equity investment which means the agencies loan you the money to make your production and if the project generates income, you pay them back on a proportional basis. Even though it might not sound attractive to you to have someone sharing in the profits, these organizations typically provide the largest portion of the program's budget.

Government Funding– A Competitive Process

These agencies all have excellent websites where you can find out more information on how to apply, and in some cases you can download the application forms from the website. Or you can call and speak to your old friend the receptionist or secretary and find out how to get more information.

Television Industry Funds

Another important source of funding for television is from industry funds set up by private or not-for-profit organizations in the

Industry Funds

television industry. There are many of them and their mandates vary widely in terms of what types of programming they will fund. Some funds only specialize in children's programming while other funds specialize in documentary funding and so on. Again, most of these industry funds have wonderful websites which will explain everything. Applications to these funds are also very competitive and it helps to have experience as a producer before applying.

Arts Councils

A Place for New Producers

Every province in Canada has an arts council that provides funding for artistic endeavors and some of them will make funds available for television programming. In this case you will probably find funding for television classified as 'video.' Arts councils often have strict guidelines as to what type of videos they will fund with the usual stipulation being that the project must be highly artistic in nature and must not be made for commercial purposes. This is the only time you don't have to have a broadcast license to be able to apply for funding. In fact, some arts councils will not allow you to have a broadcast license at all.

Arts-Council Format

You will have to change your proposal quite a bit to make it applicable to the arts-council format. They will provide you with guidelines on what type of proposal to send in, with the treatment being of primary importance. The arts councils are there to foster creation of the arts so they are going to be very interested in your proposed creative treatment of the project. These councils are excellent places for new producers to find funding.

Foundations

There are hundreds of charitable foundations throughout Canada. These are organizations whose mandate it is to give out money. Some of these foundations will donate money to television productions if the producer is associated with a non-profit, charitable organization. Check the foundations guidelines; not all foundations want you to be associated with a charitable organization but this is almost always the criteria. To be associated with a charitable organization you have to find one that would be interested in your project because it fits their mandate. For example, if you were making a documentary about children with diabetes, the Canadian Diabetes Association might be interested in helping you to raise money for your documentary or at least allow you to be associated with their organization.

Associate Your Interest with Their Mandate

Some provincial educational broadcasters also have charitable status and if you have a broadcast license with them, you may ask permission to be classified under their charitable status.

Only certain types of television projects are eligible to apply to foundations. Projects such as documentaries, children's programming, and some dramas that deal with serious issues, such as social issues, might be eligible to apply.

The Research Routine

These foundations will fund productions that mirror their organizational mandate. The best place to research mandates is in the *Canadian Directory to Foundations*, a reference book that can be purchased from the Canadian Centre for Philanthropy in Toronto or can be found in most public libraries.

Like the arts councils, the proposal you send to foundations needs to be modified to fit their criteria, which usually involves a concentration on the educational aspects of your project.

Government Branches

I have classified this area of financing as "Government Branches," not to be confused with the previous heading "Government Funding Agencies." The sole mandate of government funding agencies is to fund projects in the entertainment industry, while government branches are your regular run-of-the-mill government departments that take care of everything from heritage conservation to old-age pensions.

Let's take heritage conservation for example. If you were doing a series about Canadian history, you would contact the Department of Canadian Heritage which is part of the federal government and has several programs that fund television programs.

To find out about these government branches look in the blue pages section of the phone book as it lists all government branches. Then do the usual research routine of calling or surfing the net to check out their priorities.

Interest Groups

Like foundations, there are hundreds of interest groups and associations throughout Canada that might be interested in placing money in your production. These range from small gatherings of interested people who share a common goal to large associations that represent hundreds of members. These interest groups might be keen on a television project if your program matches their mandate. For example, if we go back to the example about the documentary on children with diabetes, you may find that there is an association called Parents of Children with Diabetes that may be willing to give you funds. Obviously the smaller the group, the less money they will give, but don't discount their worth as they may be able to introduce you to similar groups. You will be surprised to learn that there are interest groups covering every bizarre and obscure area you can think of. So look around, you'll eventually find one to suit your project. I was surprised once to see in the credits of a drama about civil war in Latin America, that it was funded by the Anarchists' Convention. Wouldn't their meetings be interesting?

The Worth of Small Groups

While we're on the subject of credits, a very important tip is to watch the end-credits of projects similar to yours to see who funded the project. Names of these organizations will be listed under the headings "with the participation of," "supported by," or some other similar phrase. These are places you should try because if they have supported projects similar to yours in the past, they may do so again.

Sponsors

Sponsors are essentially businesses supportive of your idea. They are generally big businesses with lots of capital. If your project would in some way match their corporate philosophy or business plan, they might be interested. They might also be interested if your project is going to be high quality because sponsors like to be associated with quality productions.

Corporate Sponsorship

If you remember back to the glory days of television, companies like General Electric and Ford used to sponsor dramatic series, and they still do, so if you're lucky you might be able to convince a corporate sponsor to invest in your project. I must warn you that sponsors are a hard sell, as it is difficult to get them to part with their money. Corporate sponsors are incredibly savvy about television, and are generally only interested in high profile programs that bring in substantial number of viewers. They have audience ratings and television marketing down to a science. What you might try to do is target small- to medium-sized businesses as every producer tries to interest large companies such as General Electric and Ford.

The proposal you send to each company will have to be modified to reflect how that company would benefit from being a sponsor of your program. You must first check with the television broadcaster who is going to air your program before accepting sponsorship funds because some broadcasters will not allow sponsorship on their network or may have strict guidelines on how you can acknowledge the participation of your sponsor during the program.

Even though finding sponsors is a hard sell there are some producers who do it quite successfully. Some producers are able to find enough sponsors to fund a whole series of programs. There is also a method of getting a broadcast license whereby the producer buys the airtime from the broadcaster and airs the program filled with the sponsor's commercials.

Modify Your Proposal

Tax Credits

Tax credits are a very important part of putting together the Canadian financing for your project. In Canada, producers get tax credits on wages paid to Canadian workers; the tax credit is tied to labour expenses. This means that when your production is completed, you are entitled to get money back on a percentage of the money you paid out in salaries to Canadian workers.

Canadian Tax Credits

There are two types of tax credits: the federal and provincial. The federal tax credit is a rebate on labour expenses paid to Canadian workers. The provincial tax credit is a rebate paid on labour expenses paid to Canadian workers who

Federal and Provincial Tax Credits

reside in the province where the program was filmed. For example, if I was producing a drama in British Columbia, using BC crew and actors, and my company was based in BC, I would first be eligible to receive the federal tax credit because everyone working on the project is Canadian. Next I would be able to receive the British Columbia tax credit as all of the crew and actors were BC residents. Now, to take this a step further, if this project was being made by me based in British Columbia in co-operation with another producer from Ontario, and some of the work was being done in both provinces, we could access the federal tax credit, the BC tax credit, plus the Ontario tax credit.

Getting the Paperwork Done

Now keep in mind, this is financing that is received months after the project is completed. The other drawback is the paperwork for the tax credits can be very time-consuming, but this is money you are entitled to so doing a little work is worth it. Thankfully there are consultants who specialize in preparing tax credit returns so they can do the work for you. To find out about the federal tax credit, contact the Canadian Audio-Visual Certification Office (CAVCO) based in Ottawa and for information about provincial tax credits, call the government funding agencies who fund television programming in each province.

Deferrals

The Producer Doesn't Get Paid

This is a word most producers don't like to use because it usually translates to "the producer doesn't get paid." As explained earlier, in a deferral situation, someone working on your project (the producer, crew member, or supplier), agrees not to get paid up front but will wait to get paid when money is available or the project is completed. It is usually the producer who defers his or her salary. Sometimes the director or crew members will also agree to a deferral or suppliers such as equipment houses or editing facilities will agree to defer payment for their work until all other expenses have been paid.

Deferral of wages is something you only want to do in desperate circumstances. Of course you want to get paid and so does everyone else, but the entertainment business is the only business where you will see people agree to work on a project on a deferral basis because they believe in it, or they want experience, or for various other reasons.

A Last Resort

I often think that being in the entertainment business is a lifestyle choice, not a career choice. A lot of people get into it because they have the passion and the desire to translate an idea to the screen; they don't necessarily do it because they think they are going to make a lot of money.

The Entertainment Business: A Lifestyle Choice

I should dispel one myth right away. Don't expect to makes lots of money being a producer in Canada. Producers may make a lot of money in the United States, but there simply isn't that type of money to be made in Canada. Be prepared to settle down for the long-run because it might be a long time before you see any money for yourself as producer of your project.

Interim Financing

Interim financing is just what the name suggests, it is temporary financing for the times when you don't have money leveraged against the times you do have money. This type of financing is available through banks who have entertainment divisions and through larger companies in the entertainment business.

Guaranteed Sources
of Income

This type of financing is only available in cases where producers already have guaranteed sources of income for their project that are set to come in at certain stages in the production process and are not necessarily available when needed. For example, broadcasters will not give you the total amount of the license fee up front because they want to be sure you will not abscond with their money. They will pay you the license fee in stages such as a quarter when you sign a contract, another quarter when you start principal photography (filming), a third quarter when you present them with a rough cut (draft) of the program, and the last quarter when you deliver the completed program.

Financing
The Dry Spells

So there will be times when you are going to need money but the money you have been promised is not due to come for several months. In this case, you may wish to seek interim financing. It's basically a loan to carry through the dry spells when you are short of money. You will pay interest fees in exchange for the use of the money.

Distributors

Sometimes, if you're very lucky, you might be able to get a distributor to give you a distribution advance for your project. Distributors are people who sell your finished product to television stations, educational facilities, airlines, army bases and to anyone else to whom they can sell your program in Canada and around the world. They essentially sell it when the project is completed but sometimes if they really believe in the project, they might be willing to give you money as an advance against future sales. Unfortunately, you can't find many Canadian television distributors who do this but if you're a shrewd negotiator, and your project is highly marketable, you might have some success. The best way to find Canadian distributors is to call Telefilm Canada, ask for their list of approved television distributors and find those who distribute products similar to yours.

Distribution Advance

American/Foreign Co-producers

American/Foreign co-producers are television broadcasters around the globe who might be interested in giving you a television broadcast license to air your program in their area of the world. It is the same as the Canadian broadcast license except it's for different territories. When Canadian broadcasters agree to air your program, they only broadcast it in Canada, leaving the rest of the world open. The entertainment industry is one of the areas where you

American/Foreign Broadcast License

Television: All About
Selling Territories

can make a single product and sell that product to people around the world. As a metaphor, if I were to make a fabulous new soft drink and sell you a can, I would wait for you to take a sip, take it out of your hands, and then sell it to numerous other people around the world. Television is all about selling territories. If you have a good program, you can sell it to different countries around the world.

Private Investors

These are people we all hope to know, people with money who would like to invest in your project. In some cases it may be family members, in other cases it may be wealthy individuals who have extra money to spend. Sometimes these people invest in the entertainment industry because they don't mind taking a risk and possibly because they like the glamour of being associated with a television production.

Few and Far Between

Private investors are few and far between. Of course, some producers are very adept at finding private investors. Whether through family or business connections, they are able to finance their entire production through private investment. But for most producers, this is a hard way to find financing because the producer cannot guarantee the investor a return on their investment, or even that they will get their money back. In television it is virtually impossible to predict whether your investors will make a profit.

You may be lucky enough to make many pre-sales (sales made before the project is completed) to broadcasters, distributors, or to whomever else you are selling to, and thus be able to predict a profit, but nine times out of ten you will not know whether or not you have a hit program on your hands that will generate profit.

Presales

An Ideal World

In an ideal world, you could raise financing for your project from all of these sources and more. I have only provided you with a selection of ways to find television financing. If you're enterprising, you will think up more formulas. You are only limited by your imagination and your ability to sell yourself and your idea.

Who Will Be Interested In Your Project?

The best thing you can do after you've written your proposal and ascertained that your idea is marketable, is to sit down and think hard about all the places you might find funding. Think to yourself, who in this world would be interested in this project? Keep in mind that most of your financing will come from Canadian sources but don't limit yourself to Canada, think about all the possibilities.

Just be realistic in your approach; just because you think you have a great idea doesn't mean that everyone else will agree. Always keep your feet on the ground and your head out of the clouds.

Checklist

In order to make it easier for you to plan your financing strategy, here is a list of the possible avenues to try.

1. National Television Broadcasters
2. Provincial Television Broadcasters
3. Government Funding Agencies
4. Television Industry Funds
5. Arts Councils
6. Foundations
7. Government Branches
8. Interest Groups
9. Sponsors
10. Tax Credits
11. Deferrals
12. Interim Financing
13. Distributors
14. American/Foreign Co-producers
15. Private Investors

Chapter Four

Finding the Holy Grail—What to do When the Money Comes In

Now that you've sent off your proposal, you face the real test of whether your idea is good or not. As instructed in the previous chapter, you sent your proposal to broadcasters first. Now that you've waited a few weeks and have received rejection letters or, the miracle of all miracles, a call from a broadcaster, you are able to judge how well received your proposal has been.

If broadcasters are interested, they will likely call you for more information. Broadcasters usually call to find out more about your financing scenario, delivery date, to ask for further information about you, or for a demo tape. They are mainly concerned with your ability to raise funds for the project and your experience as a producer. Be sure to send whatever information they request right away.

Broadcasters Call for More Information

When I worked for broadcasters, I cannot tell you how many times I had called producers to ask for more information and been promised that they would send it right away, only to have the material never show up. These producers were 'just fishing.' They were inexperienced and put together a proposal to see if anyone was interested. Due to lack of experience or for some other reason, they never intended to go ahead with the project or they panicked once they realized that they might actually have to produce the project.

Do everyone a favour, yourself and the organizations you are approaching; don't waste everyone's time by 'going fishing.' Only submit your proposal if you are one hundred percent confident that you can raise the funds for your production, and have the capability and tenacity to produce a good program.

Broadcaster's Offer

After you have sent the information the broadcaster is looking for, you will again have to wait several weeks or months. With any luck, the broadcaster will come back to you with an offer. The offer will usually be a set price paid for your type of project. You can try to negotiate a higher fee but this is generally akin to pulling teeth. The broadcaster may agree to pay more if you have a good product and you're quite a talker.

The Deal Memo

Next they will send you a commitment letter, —sometimes called a deal memo—which is a brief letter stating the terms and price you have mutually agreed upon. In time this will be followed by a long-form contract. A word to the wise, never believe that any project is going to get off the ground until you receive a long-form contract.

The unfortunate drawback to the entertainment industry is that you can run into people who promise you money and then never deliver.

There could be many good reasons that they don't deliver, such as circumstances beyond their control. But if more people placed emphasis on personal integrity, the producer wouldn't be left in the cold.

Needless to say, this scenario sometimes happens. This applies to all money promised by broadcasters or other investors. You can only be assured that the money will get to you once both parties have signed a contract. Even the commitment letter does not assure you money. I have often seen projects that appeared to have one hundred percent committed funds fall apart at the last minute. Conversely, I have seen projects that were dead in the water resurrect themselves and go on to become fine productions.

Perseverance

There is just no telling what will happen to your project. I can tell you that I once had a project that looked certain to get a broadcast license only to be told at the last minute that another producer, who had significantly more financing than I did, had proposed the same idea and had been awarded the license. This, of course, was heartbreaking news for me but I calmly told the broadcaster that I was going to try to find another broadcaster for my project. This unwillingness to give up convinced the broadcaster to give me a chance and I did get the license and proceeded with the project.

It has often been my experience that those producers who keep coming back and keep plugging away no matter what the odds are the

Swallow Your Pride

producers who are going to get their project made. They have fierce personal determination to realize their dreams. Having said that, I must return you to the first chapter where I advised you to make sure your idea was marketable. Unfortunately, no matter how hard you try, an unmarketable idea will stay that way. Sometimes you have to swallow your pride. There are times you will find that you have to modify your idea or go back to the drawing board.

The Pitch

Be realistic about your project. While pitching your project to broadcasters, investors, or friends, you will run into people who will think that your project sounds great. Do not get overly confident that this appreciation will translate into hard cash. Just because investors say that they like a project does not mean they will automatically come up with funds. I once attended a television market where I met with ten potential broadcasters and investors who all said they loved my project and would definitely be interested. When it came down to actually doing business with me, only one came through with a contract.

Having cautioned you not to believe everything you're told, it is in your best interest to push the broadcaster and other investors to send you a long-form agreement as soon as possible. Some investors, such as foundations and sponsors, don't have a contract for you to sign, they will only send you a commitment letter. They generally follow this letter up with a cheque. Without sounding too greedy, always push for the money, or the contract, as soon as possible.

If you get a provincial broadcaster on board, they will send you a contract that is usually two to three pages in length and in very simple terms. The national broadcast contract is much longer. It can run several pages and if you're unfamiliar with contracts, it would be a good idea to have a lawyer look it over so you understand what you're signing.

Clauses in A Broadcast License

These are the usual clauses you will encounter in a broadcast license:

Producer is responsible for all costs of production. The broadcaster will only pay the portion of the license fee that was mutually agreed upon and not a penny more. The producer is at all times responsible for all costs associated with the production and it doesn't matter how far over budget you go, the broadcaster will not pay any further fees.

Costs of Production

Producer will complete the project based on the program concept. The broadcaster wants to make sure that you are going to deliver the program they agreed to buy. It is often the case that elements of the story get changed in the production process. This is to be expected as long as the changes are not going to radically redesign the concept you originally presented. If you feel that the concept is totally changing, you must contact the broadcaster for their prior

Program Concept

approval. Otherwise, you may find that the broadcaster feels that you have changed the terms of the contract and will not pay the rest of the license fee.

Producer shall obtain industry-standard insurance. There are two types of insurance that a broadcaster normally insists that you buy: production insurance, and errors and omissions insurance.

Production Insurance

Production insurance is coverage that provides for any mishaps that happen on set. For example, should you ruin a carpet in the house you are shooting in while on location or damage one of the lights you rented from an equipment house, production insurance would cover the resulting claims.

Errors and Omissions Insurance

Errors and omissions insurance covers any potential lawsuits that arise over the broadcast or promotion of the project. For example, should you interview a policeman who doesn't like the way his comments were portrayed when he sees it on television and decides to take you to court, the errors and omissions insurance would help to pay for legal fees.

As a deterrent to potential lawsuits, you must get anyone who appears in your production to sign a release form. In the case of paid actors, a contract is signed. Essentially, the release form states that the interviewee or actor agrees to be in the production and will not sue you in the future. Be cautious though, just because a person signs a release form doesn't mean they can't sue you. Anyone can sue you for anything no matter what they have signed. Whether they win or not is another matter.

The entertainment world is a very litigious area, possibly because the public rightly or wrongly believes that there is a lot of money to be made in television. They are propelled by the fact they may get some of that money from you if they threaten to sue.

Litigious Entertainment World

Unfortunately, I have experienced many situations where a participant in a production has asked for money that he/she was not entitled to or has claimed that he/she owned rights to material that the producer wanted to use. Be cautious; when producing for television, realize that you might run into problems such as these. To counteract this possibility, make sure that you have release forms, proper clearances, and music rights before allowing your program to be broadcast.

Most producers incorporate a new company for each project, sometimes called a 'single-purpose company.' The sole purpose of this company is to produce the project; the corporation is folded when the project is finished. Producers do this for tax reasons as well as to limit any liability should a legal claim arise. Always hire a lawyer to discuss any legal issues because the amount you pay in legal fees now could save you from a legal nightmare in the future.

The Single-Purpose Company

Original Concept

The producer warrants that they own all rights to the concept as well as all music rights. The broadcaster wants to be sure that this is your original concept, that you didn't steal it from anyone, and that you aren't using music you don't have the rights to use.

Editing—Fear Not!

The broadcaster shall have the right to approve components of the project. These components can include personnel, budget, scripts, rough cut (first draft), fine cut (completed program) and credits. The broadcaster can request that you change many items in your production. Generally, broadcasters take a hands-off approach and don't interfere with the creative process, but sometimes you get a broadcaster who wants editorial input. There is not much you can do about this except work with the broadcaster and be open to their suggestions. After all, they are paying thousands of dollars for your project and they deserve input.

Be Professional

The broadcaster may edit the program for scheduling and timing requirements. Each broadcaster has a certain length of program they like to air because each is allowed to broadcast a varying number of commercials. Because of this, the broadcaster may need to edit your program to fit their schedule. The broadcaster may give you the choice of editing the project yourself or editing it in consultation with them. If you are not given a choice, don't worry as the broadcaster will only edit portions of the program that are minor and will not want to fool with the creative look of the project.

A representative of the broadcaster has the right to be present during the production period. This is strictly a fall-back measure for the broadcaster in case it looks like you're not going to deliver the program. I have yet to hear of a situation in Canada where a broadcaster was on-set breathing down the producer's neck. I am sure that you realize that once you take a broadcaster's money, you must deliver the program. Always be professional and deliver what you say you are going to deliver or, as the saying goes, "You'll never eat lunch in this town again."

Broadcasters' Fall-Back Measure

The end credits shall be subject to the broadcaster's approval. Broadcasters want to be sure that their name is prominently featured at the end of the program. This is where they get publicity in exchange for their investment. It's similar to when you go to see a film. All of those people left in the dark theater at the end of the film watching the credits are probably in the entertainment industry. Watching the credits gets to be a habit; you want to see if you recognize any names, organizations and, of course, you want to find out where the producer got the financing. The broadcaster wants to ensure that he or she gets the proper credit, so it will always be the broadcaster's contractual right to approve the end credits.

Watch The Credits

The producer will supply the broadcaster with a submaster of the program and will store the master in a secure location which can be made accessible to the broadcaster upon proper notification. A submaster is a duplicate of the

Master and Sub-master Copies

original copy of the program which is called the master. You always want to keep the master copy of the program for yourself in a safe, dry location. Can you imagine if anything happened to this copy? All the time and effort you put into making it would be destroyed. The broadcaster should always have access to the master in case the submaster is misplaced or is of poor quality and they need to make another copy. Never give the broadcaster your master copy to air.

Music Cue Sheets

Producer shall deliver music cue sheets to broadcaster. Music cue sheets are sheets of paper that list all the information about the music contained in your project. These sheets list the titles of the musical compositions plus the name of the composer or artist and so on. The broadcaster has to submit these sheets to SOCAN, the organization that remits music royalties to musicians and composers.

Exclusive and Non-exclusive Rights

Producer grants broadcaster the exclusive rights to broadcast the program for x number of years in abc territories and thereafter the non-exclusive rights to broadcast the program for x number of years. This goes back to the theory of first and second windows. The broadcaster who has paid the most money is entitled to the first window and to air the program exclusively in their territory for a certain length of time. After the exclusive run, they are allowed to broadcast the project non-exclusively for another length of time during which other broadcasters may air it simultaneously. It is in the producer's best interest if the exclusive period is one year or less.

The broadcaster will try to negotiate a longer exclusive period for themselves, so this involves a bit of bargaining. Generally, broadcast licenses run for five years with a portion of the license being exclusive and the rest being non-exclusive.

The producer grants to broadcaster xyz non-broadcast rights. Some broadcasters want certain non-broadcast rights in return for their investment. These rights could include home video rights, CD-ROM and other multimedia rights such as those for the internet, educational, and the list goes on. They should technically pay you extra for these non-broadcast rights but some broadcasters automatically consider internet rights, for example, to be part of their broadcast license.

Non-Broadcast Rights

You should look closely at the non-broadcast rights the broadcaster is requesting. In most cases you wouldn't want to give these rights up as you may want to exploit them yourself or ask a distributor who specializes in selling rights to sell them for you.

The program shall be certified as Canadian and the producer shall remit to the broadcaster the Canadian content certification number. By law, all Canadian broadcasters must broadcast a certain percentage of Canadian-produced programs, giving them an incentive to buy from Canadian producers. The broadcaster wants to ensure that your program will be considered Canadian so you must apply to the Canadian Radio-television and Telecommunications

Canadian Content

Commission (CRTC), based in Ottawa, for a Canadian certification number. As long as the majority of your crew, cast and essential personnel are Canadian, and your storyline was developed and substantially written by Canadians, the certification process will be painless.

Key Personnel

The producer shall notify the broadcaster of any changes which affect key personnel or production elements. The broadcaster wants to ensure that the key personnel you presented as working on the production will continue to work for the duration of the production. If there are any changes to personnel or production elements such as storyline, the broadcaster will want to know. They are mostly concerned that the production will run smoothly and that the producer or director is not going to quit half way through and therefore jeopardize the production.

Raising the Rest of the Money

If all looks well with the contract and you have a lawyer look it over, sign it and be happy, as you have passed the first step in realizing your project. Now you have to raise the rest of the money. Many new producers become totally confused by the financing process because securing a broadcaster is the essential first step in producing a program, but it is often difficult to get a broadcaster if you don't have other funds secured first. It becomes a Catch-22 situation where the broadcaster doesn't want to be the first investor, but no one else will invest unless you have a broadcast license.

In this scenario the best option is to apply to funding schemes such as arts councils, where you don't need a broadcaster, or to send your proposal to broadcasters and other investors who might write you a letter of interest saying that if you find a portion of your financing, they might invest later on. Then you can use these letters in your proposal to show investors that you do have outside interest, you just need their support to begin and the rest of the money will follow.

If you are a new producer, you will find that getting your first project off the ground is very difficult. No one wants to invest in you because you have no experience. This will be the hardest test you will go through as it generally gets easier to find investors and broadcasters as you gain experience.

Securing the First Investment

Let's assume that you have secured a broadcast license. Now is the time to submit your proposal to other investors. State in your cover letter and finance plan that you do have a broadcaster, and hopefully the potential investor will look more favourably upon your application. You will find it hardest to secure the first investment, however after you do get it, you will find that other investments begin trickling in.

Generally, after receiving the broadcast license you will apply to government funding agencies. Their application forms are usually complex and involve handing in a lot of support material. There are some consultants who, for a

Applying To Government Funding Agencies

fee, will help you to fill out these application forms. After filling them out and waiting an extraordinary amount of time, you may be lucky to receive funding. As the contracts used by these agencies are usually voluminous and complicated, it is a good idea to have a lawyer read them over.

Equity Investment

As mentioned previously, funds received from government agencies generally take the form of equity investment, meaning that you will have to pay the money back. The attractiveness to applying to government funding agencies is the large amount of funds they invest but the drawback is that you will have to report, as well as remit funds, to these agencies for years after the project is finished. Next, you can apply to any of the myriad of funding agencies and investors you can think of.

Deciding When To Begin Production

Now that you have received funds you have to decide when to begin production. Some producers begin once they have received the majority of their financing or at least enough to begin the principal photography stage. In some cases, if you can tell investors you have started filming and are able to show them footage, investors who were reluctant before may now invest, the theory being that if you've come this far, you are bound to finish. Most projects will fail in the fundraising and development stage because at this point, the producer has not invested too much money and it is still possible to back out. Once you have started filming, you have invested too much time and money to quit.

The thought of being a failure is always a good incentive to finish a project. At this point, producers will do anything to finish the project and will miraculously scrape the necessary money together.

Be Confident

Other producers will only begin production once the entire budget has been raised. It just depends on your personal tolerance for risk. You may be someone who believes strongly in what you are doing and will take a risk and begin filming in the hope that money will come in later. Or you may be the cautious sort and wait for all of the funds to be raised. Whatever your choice, understand that in a situation where you haven't raised any funds and you decide to pay for the production yourself, you are taking a huge risk. Don't ever hold out hope that by some miracle at the end of production investors will be so impressed by what they see that they will happily give you funds. This is an unrealistic expectation and will cause you to go into debt.

Whatever choice you make, if you are confident in your abilities your project should come to fruition.

Chapter Five

How to Make More Money—Marketing and Distribution

We will now fast-forward until your production is complete. We all know what a fantasy world television can be, so we can get away with pretending that your program or series is now finished. We will not deal with the production process as there are several fine books already written on this subject and the real business of this book is to show you how to find money. This chapter will deal with the stages that commence after production has wrapped.

Time to Think About Promotions

You have now delivered the program to your broadcasters and complimentary copies to other investors. At this point, it's wise to begin thinking about promotions. From a business standpoint, promotions are very important because any positive publicity for your current production will help to propel you further ahead in your next project. It's very hard for new producers to find investors but if you have produced before, and can place copies of reviews or articles written about your previous project in your next proposal, this will be very impressive to the potential investor.

Technically, it is the broadcaster who is supposed to promote your project but it's always wise to do some promotions of your own. You need to work in conjunction with the broadcaster's publicist and keep them informed of what you are doing, but it's the producer who has the passion for the project and who is the best person to arrange promotions.

Promotions involve contacting the press and trying to generate public awareness of your project. If you have the money, invest in hiring a good freelance publicist who will promote your program for you. They have the press contacts and know how to get free publicity. If you don't have the money then work at promoting the project yourself. Find out the names of journalists from newspapers who cover television, the arts, or other areas applicable to your production, and send them information. Before you send the information do your research on the paper and what sort of audience they reach.

Do Your Research

As with your proposal, don't send information to just any media outlet. You should send your information to journalists who may be interested in writing an article or short piece about your production, so do your research. Don't limit yourself to the big newspapers as there are also local newspapers, specialty newspapers, magazines and radio programs who may be interested in what you have produced. Sit down and think of who in Canada would be interested in writing a story about your production.

The Press Release

Once you have targeted those individuals, send them a press release which should be approximately a page to a page and a half and should contain the name of your program, the date the program will be aired and the broadcasters who are airing it. Include a short description of your program, an expanded project focus will do. Include your name, the director's name, the names of any well-known crew or actors and your phone number to call for further information. The KISS principle applies here as well—keep it short and simple.

If you think broadcasters receive a lot of proposals, the press receives this number ten-fold in the form of press releases and press kits, so you want to make your point quickly and clearly. Include with your press release a VHS cassette of the program and be sure to label the cassette with the name of the program, your name and phone number, the date of broadcast and broadcasters involved as cassettes sometimes get separated from press releases.

Production Photographs 'Stills'

If you have production photographs, more commonly referred to as 'stills' include these as well. These can be stills you took of cast and crew during the shoot or graphic images you have designed from frames of video. You can also include a high-quality photograph of yourself. All of these pictures must be top-quality, professional-looking photographs. Never send photographs that look amateurish or are of poor quality.

Above all, make sure that you send this package to the press well in advance of your program's air date. If members of the press receive your information after the air date or in the week before, there is nothing they can do with the material.

Although you have no way to gauge whether publicity attracts viewers to your program, the broadcasters are definitely able to measure the benefits of publicity. Not only do they receive daily or weekly audience ratings reports, they also subscribe to clippings services which are companies that search all of the newspapers in the country and will clip articles that mention your program. If there's been an article written about your program, the broadcasters have it. This is the tremendous business advantage to generating publicity; if the broadcaster picks up on hype surrounding your program, they will be more inclined to invest in your future projects.

Benefits of Publicity

Besides generating publicity, you want to generate income with your program. Now that you've pre-sold it to as many broadcasters as possible, it's time to look at distribution and exploiting unsold rights.

Distribution

In television there are two types of distribution, theatrical distribution and non-theatrical distribution. Non-theatrical distribution can also be referred to as 'non-commercial distribution' or 'educational distribution.' Theatrical distribution is a confusing term as it implies that your program will be shown in movie theatres, when in fact it means that distribution will be directed towards television broadcasters. Non-theatrical

Types of Distribution

distribution means that distribution will be directed towards other outlets such as educational facilities and libraries

Finding Suitable Distributors

Both types of distribution should be handled by an experienced distributor. You may decide to find one distributor who can handle both types, but it's in your best interest to have one for each type of distribution as most distributors excel in one of the two areas. Another reason to have two distributors is the fact that you have no idea how well they will distribute your program and if you don't like the sales results they are achieving, you are stuck with the distributor for at least five years, the length of a typical distribution contract.

Splitting the distribution rights between two distributors increases the level of service you receive from each and increases your chance of a good working relationship; if you're not happy with one distributor, you will hopefully be happy with the other. This is not meant to cast suspicion over your distributor, but in some cases producers feel that distributors do not adequately promote their programs to buyers as a given producer's program is usually only one of several programs the distributor has in their inventory.

It's also difficult to track a distributor's expenses, as a distributor makes money by earning a commission from any sales they make on your behalf. A distributor is also allowed to deduct expenses from money due to the producer.

These are expenses incurred while selling your production and are mainly comprised of promotional costs such as publicity flyers, advertisements, shipping fees, taxes as well as a myriad of other costs associated with selling your program.

Distribution is one area in which producers generally wish they had more control. Once you sign a contract with a distributor, they have the exclusive right to represent your production for several years. If you are not happy with the results you have no recourse except to wait out the contract.

Think Before You Sign

Thankfully, in Canada television distributors operate with a high degree of professionalism so there is no cause for alarm. You do hear of abuses taking place in the distribution of feature films, but television is an area that is generally well run. The prudent producer is best advised to find a distributor who distributes productions similar to their own, to ask the distributor for references from current clients and to investigate the distributor as best they can.

You can attempt to do the distribution yourself but this is an unwise decision. There are so many avenues for sales that even the most informed producer would not be familiar with them all, so it's best to leave distribution up to the people who know the distribution business.

Theatrical Distribution

Theatrical distribution is the route whereby

The Theatrical Route

the distributor sells your program to broad-casters in Canada and around the world. When broadcasters buy a finished program it is called an 'acquisition,' and broadcasters have set fees that they will pay for such programs. Let me warn you, acquisition prices are not high. Broadcasters don't pay anywhere near the price they pay for programs in the proposal stage. It may seem crazy that broadcasters will pay more for an incomplete program over which they have no control than they will for a finished program that they can judge immediately. The reality is that broadcasters pay more for incomplete programs, referred to as 'presales' or 'co-produc-tions,' as opposed to finished programs, known as 'acquisitions.' This way, they can get their names in the credits and possibly earn a piece of the profits.

The Theatrical Distribution Contract

When you sign an agreement with a theatrical distributor, it will stipulate that the distributor is allowed to sell your program to broadcasters around the world unless otherwise stipulated by the producer. The theatrical distribution contract will also state the right of the distributor to con-trol non-theatrical rights. As mentioned earlier, you may want to give these non-theatrical distri-bution rights to another distributor who special-izes in the area, so read the contract carefully before signing. It is perfectly acceptable for you to ask the distributor to cross out certain rights from the contract before signing. If they choose not to do so then you have the option of backing out of the deal and finding another distributor. This is where your negotiation skills come into play, as you may also want to negotiate the distributor's commission down from the level they are asking for, but like bargaining with broadcasters, this is akin to pulling teeth.

The theatrical distribution contract will also give the distributor the right to sell certain non-theatrical rights such as home video, internet, and multi-media. Think carefully before giving these rights away, especially the home video rights. If you feel that this program will sell well in the home video market, you may want to give these rights to another distributor who specializes in selling home video. This is most applicable to the children's video market in which home video sales can be quite lucrative. New producers are under the mistaken impression that there is much money to be made in the home video market—this is probably not the case. The home video market in Canada is relatively small, so big profits are rather unattainable.

The Home Video Market

Non-Theatrical Distribution

The second type of distribution, non-theatrical distribution or educational distribution, is the process by which the distributor sells the completed program to schools, libraries, airlines, military bases and any other medium that doesn't involve broadcast television. Of the two types of distribution, educational distribution reaps the smaller rewards. The reason is clear; schools and libraries simply don't have the resources to pay big fees to purchase videotapes.

The Less Lucrative Route

For both types of distribution, profits return to the producer very slowly. It takes at least sixteen months for any substantial profits to be generated. Look at it this way, it will be a happy surprise when you're toiling away on your next project and you receive a cheque from the previous project.

The Distribution Contract

Covering Your Legal Position

For either type of distribution, the producer and the distributor have to sign a distribution agreement. These are generally short agreements of a few pages that set out the parameters of rights being assigned to the distributor. These contracts can contain a lot of 'legalese' and are best shown to a lawyer. Standard clauses you find contained within a distribution agreement are:

Producer's Ownership & Authority

The producer has the power and authority to enter into this agreement and to grant all rights herein to the distributor. Most of the clauses in the distribution agreement will relate to the distributor making sure that their legal position is covered and that no one will sue them for an oversight made by the producer. In this contract, the producer is stating that they own the program free and clear and that they have the sole authority to allow distribution of the production.

Distributor's 'Exclusive' Contract

The producer grants to the distributor the exclusive right to distribute and exploit the program in abc territories and xyz forms of television for x amount of time. This translates into 'only the distributor is allowed to sell your program for the term of the contract.' The word 'exclusive' means that the distributor is the only one allowed to distribute your program in the specified territories and forms of television. This clause is usually preceded by a list of non-theatrical rights that you are granting to the distributor.

The producer warrants that he or she owns all rights in and to the program as well as material contained within the program including musical rights and that such rights will be in effect for the duration of the distribution agreement. Here, the producer is verifying that he or she owns sufficient rights to all material contained in the production for it to be distributed in the territories and time period granted to the distributor. These rights can include music rights, rights to an actor's performance, stock footage rights and so on. Ideally, the producer wants to hold worldwide rights in perpetuity to creative elements contained within the program. Producers want these rights so they can exploit the program throughout the world for a never-ending period of time and not have to concern themselves with paying extra fees in the future.

Purchasing Rights

Most producers cannot afford to pay for worldwide rights in perpetuity so they buy rights to creative elements only for a particular territory and number of years. For example, if you were going to include a top-40 hit as the theme song for your program, the rights to use the song could be very expensive. You might decide that you only have enough funds to pay for the right to broadcast the song in Canada for five years. Years later, you may decide to have your distributor distribute the program in the United States, at which time you will have to go back to the organization you obtained the music rights from and pay a 'step-up' fee in order to obtain the American rights.

No Claims, Liens or
Encumbrances

The producer warrants that there are no claims, liens or encumbrances against the program or the material on which it is based which will interfere with or hinder the rights granted to the distributor. Here, the producer is attesting that there are no legal claims against the program that could potentially stop distribution. The distributor does not want to spend time and effort trying to sell a program that the producer legally doesn't have the rights to.

Foreign Taxes

The distributor may deduct from payments due to the producer any tax or withholding tax which is applicable under law and is required to be made by the distributor. This is usually one of those clauses contained in small type at the bottom of television and distribution agreements. Most countries around the world have taxes which have to be paid upon the sale of your production. These taxes will be taken out of the revenue due the producer. Taxes are an unhappy part of doing business with a foreign country.

Sales Reports

The distributor shall provide the producer with a financial report on the distribution of the program on a quarterly/yearly basis.

The producer's share of receipts shall be forwarded by cheque with such reports. The distributor will mail a detailed report of the sales and the amount due to the producer on either a quarterly or yearly basis. This clause is usually preceded by a clause that allows the producer to review the distributor's financial record of sales upon sufficient notice or allow the producer a certain length of time in which to bring errors to the distributor's attention.

Liability Concerns

The producer agrees to indemnify and hold the distributor harmless from any liability, including legal fees, arising from any claim inconsistent with any representation made by the producer. Here, the distributor is again covering his or her legal backside by ensuring that if there are legal problems with the production, it is the producer who is going to suffer the consequences and not the distributor.

Legal Materials

The producer warrants that there will be no defamatory, libelous or otherwise unlawful material contained within the program and that the program will not infringe on any trademark, trade name, copyright, patent, literary, artistic, dramatic, right of privacy or any other right of any person, firm or corporation. The producer is again stating that he or she did not use any material in their program they were not legally allowed to use. Producers must be extremely careful with all audio or visual material contained within their production and ensure that they have not contravened any personal or corporate rights.

Errors and Omissions Insurance

The producer will deliver to the distributor copies of an errors and omissions insurance policy. Errors and omissions insurance was previously explained as insurance that would help pay for any legal costs incurred while defending a legal suite brought against the program. In order to obtain E&O insurance, you will have to have a lawyer review the final edit of the program to let you know if there are any potential legal problems. The distributor will want proof of the existence of this insurance before they will agree to distribute the program.

International Sales

The producer agrees to supply to the distributor all audio and video materials necessary to fulfill international sales. The distributor needs the producer to supply copies of the program as well as specially prepared copies of the production containing items such as designated music and effects tracks, textless graphics and so on. The distributor will provide you with a list of the necessary items and your editor will be able to help you put together the requested tapes.

Attracting Buyers

The producer shall supply to the distributor all promotional materials for the program including stills and written material from which the distributor can create publicity materials. Just as photographs and stills are handy for publicity targeted to the press, these materials will be very useful to the distributor when trying to attract buyers. These images can be used to create brochures, flyers and advertisements.

Other Avenues of Revenue

Other Ancillary Rights. Now that you've found a distributor for theatrical and non-theatrical distribution, it's time to look at other potential avenues of revenue. One often overlooked area of rights in Canada is versioning the production into either English or French.

Versioning. If your project was completed in the English language and you have not already sold your program to a French language broadcaster in Quebec, this may be a good time to ask your theatrical distributor if they think a sale to Quebec is feasible. The converse applies to French-language programs made in Quebec. When you pre-sell your project to broadcasters during the proposal stage, the broadcaster is in most cases only purchasing the English-language rights, leaving the French-language rights free. If the program is suitable for translation, you may have a chance of selling it to a French-language broadcaster. It is to your advantage to have your distributor arrange for the language translation as the government, through Telefilm Canada, will pay for a portion of the translation costs.

French-Language Rights–A Window of Opportunity

Most programs do not translate well into another language. If the program has a large concentration of dialogue, it will have to be subtitled which is not attractive to viewers who, for the most part, do not like to read subtitles. In order for the program to translate well into another language, it has to be explained largely through actions, for example through dance, or has to be narrated through voice-over as in the case of nature programs in which you hear an announcer describing the action on the screen.

Translation Issues

Radio Opportunity

Radio. Radio is also another often overlooked ancillary right and unfortunately one that is not easily attainable. In some cases you may be able to take the audio from your production and create a radio documentary or drama. This can be quite tricky and you will want to hire an audio engineer or someone who has previously produced for radio. Only certain radio outlets are interested in acquiring material of this sort as many stations are only licensed to play music, but there are stations on the AM dial which may be interested. Be aware that prices paid for radio programs are not very high.

Multimedia Formats

Multimedia. Multimedia is another avenue to exploit in your production. This could involve making CD-roms, video games or other multimedia formats based on material from your production.   Again, not all productions will translate well into multimedia formats and if you are not familiar with multimedia, hire someone who is. Thoroughly investigate the profit potential before investing money in multimedia as there might not be a sufficient recoupment on your investment. There are, however, funds that will invest in the multimedia portion of your program just as there are television industry funds

Merchandising—
A Stroke of Luck

Merchandising. Merchandising is the sale of products related to your production. Examples are books, toys, clothing, stationery, games, print materials, home videos, interactive or multimedia products and soundtrack recordings.

You would have to be a very lucky producer in order to have a hit program which would involve merchandising. Merchandising in Canada is generally used in conjunction with children's programming.

Retransmission Rights. This is an area of revenue that most producers are not aware of. If you have a program airing on television, you may be entitled to retransmission royalties that are collected on your behalf by retransmission collectives. These are organizations that track when your project is aired and forward any fees to the producer. Basically, cable and satellite companies pay for retransmission fees which gives them the right to pick up your program and air it via cable or satellite.

Retransmission Collectives

There are retransmission collectives around the world, so if your project is being internationally distributed, sign up with all of the collectives. The revenue return on retransmission royalties is only significant if your program has been widely distributed and is often repeated or if you have many episodes in your series, however there is no cost for you to sign up with retransmission collectives. They make back their costs by charging a small administrative fee. For further information about collectives, contact the Canadian Retransmission Collective based in Toronto.

A Perfect Scenario –Ambitious But Plausible

An Ideal World. In an ideal world, you would have been able to sell all of the theatrical, non-theatrical and ancillary rights listed in this chapter plus any others you can think of. You would also have been able to access production funds utilizing the fundraising methods discussed in chapter three. To demonstrate the ideal situation for generating funding plus revenue from a production, let's go back to our documentary about the hibernation of bears from the first chapter.

National Broadcaster: At the proposal stage, we were able to sell this one-hour documentary to the Discovery Channel, which purchased the exclusive national English-language Canadian rights, gaining the right to broadcast the program coast to coast across Canada, excluding Quebec.

Provincial Broadcasters: Also at the proposal stage, we were able to sell the program to provincial broadcasters across the country in British Columbia, Saskatchewan, Alberta, Ontario, Nova Scotia and the Northwest Territories.

English/French-Language Versioning: As this documentary contains a lot of footage of bears in the wild and is narrated through voice-over, it can be easily translated. This program was originally made in English but as we were able to translate it into French, we sold it in proposal stage to a broadcaster in Quebec.

Fundraising for Production: Once we had found as many broadcasters as we could find at the proposal stage, we went to industry and government funds where we were able to successfully raise financing.

Sponsorship: We then took our proposal plus a demo tape to a company who makes honey and who decided to come on board as an official sponsor if we named them in the credits.

Foundations: We then approached a foundation that raises awareness about the need to save wildlife habitats and we were able to obtain a grant.

Interest Groups: Luckily, the foundation we received the grant from told us about a Canadian group that raises public awareness of the need to protect wild bears and they were able to give us a donation.

American Broadcaster: As we had the Canadian Discovery Channel on board, it was not difficult to sell the program to the American Discovery Channel for the right to broadcast it in the United States.

Private Investor: One of our uncles who is an environmentalist felt that this would be a worthwhile cause to donate a few thousand dollars to.

Distributor: Now that the documentary has been completed, we have found a theatrical distributor who will sell it to broadcasters around the world. We have also found a non-theatrical distributor who will distribute the program to schools and libraries. Because we felt that this documentary would do well in home video sales, we have given the home video rights to another distributor who specializes in the home video market.

Tax Credits: Several months after the completion of the production we applied for the federal tax credit because all crew members were Canadian and our company is based in British Columbia using B.C. labour so we were able to apply for the B.C. tax credit.

Radio: During production of the documentary we interviewed scientists who talked about the unique aspects of the hibernation of bears. We were able to take some of these interviews plus sound bites of the bears and make a fifteen minute radio documentary.

Multimedia: We were able to take some of the material from the documentary and turn it into an educational CD rom for which we found a distributor who would ensure it was marketed toward schools.

Merchandising: As the documentary featured cuddly bears, we were able to make lunchpails featuring a picture of the bears and sell it through a large department store.

Retransmission Collectives: When we could not think of any further areas of revenue, we signed up for every retransmission collective we could find and will wait until sometime next year to see a cheque.

This may seem like an ambitious scenario but it is totally plausible. Don't get discouraged if you can't attain even a fraction of this scenario. Selling in all of these markets is very difficult and takes a lot of patience and a very good product, but it's nice to know that everything is possible.

So Where Do I Go From Here?

Now that you've completed your program or series and have exploited all of the areas of revenue you felt were exploitable, it's time to think of the future. If your production was very successful there may be future areas for expansion, for example prequels, sequels, movies of the week and feature films. Please understand that it is difficult to have a hit program that will successfully create spin-offs. In television, everything is possible but this is a once-in-a-lifetime shot.

Financing Plus Reality

You have probably figured out that this book is trying to offer you tips on financing plus a healthy dose of reality. Even though I encourage you to explore your project's potential, I also want you to understand that you have to be realistic in your goals. Being a television producer is very hard and sometimes you lose more money than you make. So be cautious and proceed with what you're capable of handling. If you have to start small then so be it, use your first production as a lever to something bigger and better next time.

Future Expansion

Chapter Six

How to Fake it in TV

Now that you have read all the advice and followed all the instructions, it's time to call yourself a producer. I have often joked that there are a lot of producers out there who shouldn't be called producers, so on their behalf I set out to write an article entitled *How to Fake it in TV*. This tongue-in-cheek article explains the easy way to make it in the television industry. It contains tips on how to be devious, mischievous, and conniving by using creative phrasing and shameless self-promotion. The beginning of the article is contained below. It's pure fiction, but within it you'll find examples drawn from everyday life in the television industry.

Real Life Advice On How to Fake it in TV

In television, there are many big players controlling the deals and producing the programs. So what do you do if you're a small fish in a big pond? You may not have connections or experience, but you want to make it as a producer. Live by these rules, follow this advice, and the next big success could be yours:

1. Write a producer's bio for yourself to impress people with your experience. Of course, you have no experience but don't let that deter you. Simply write down the name of every video production you have ever made. It can even be one you shot in film school or made fooling around with a camcorder. It doesn't matter if these productions were not professionally produced or do not have a proper title—make one up! For example:

I have enjoyed a long and varied career in producing. Previous productions include
Road Hockey: When to Shout "Car"
and
White Balance Your Camera: A Nightmare.

2. In your bio, you should also mention all the productions you hope to be making, just make up interesting titles with big words. For example:

I have several projects in development including:
Unspoilt Beaches of Bali
and
Death by Chocolate Icecream.

3. In your bio use creative phrasing to liven up otherwise boring or insignificant-sounding experience to make yourself sound extra-ordinary, for example:

This past year I was cinematographer on several Canadian productions which were filmed in and around Canada.
Translation: As I was one of the only people with a camcorder who could shoot straight, several of my friends asked me to videotape their wedding ceremonies.

4.   Tell everyone, especially the press, how a big star is considering appearing in your production when in reality all you have done is contact his or her agent who hung up on you.

Quote to the press: *Mel Gibson is being approached about starring in the leading role.*

5.   Again, leak to the press how a big-name director is considering directing your project when in reality all you have done is left a message with his or her agent. For example:

Steven Spielberg is looking at this project very seriously and is considering it alongside other projects.

6. Leave a message on your answering machine that makes you sound busy and important.

Hi. I can't come to the phone right now as I'm on-set discussing details with the crew. Leave your name and number at the tone and I'll call you back at my convenience.

7. Use the telephone to demonstrate your importance.   Arrange to have a friend call your cell phone during lunch meetings and pretend that you're putting a big deal on hold in order to continue your lunch appointment.

During lunch: *Excuse me Mr. Big, my cellphone is ringing "Hello...No I can't make it to the office right now to sign that $500,000 cheque, I'm having lunch with Mr. Big."*

8. At the close of industry seminars or workshops, rush to the nearest wall of phones and pretend that you're calling your office to check for important messages.

> *"I'm sorry Mr. Big, I can't stop and talk right now as I have to call my assistant to collect all my messages. I'm expecting a call from Fox Television."*

9. When people ask you what the budget of your last project was, inflate the budget, no matter how low it might have been, by at least one hundred percent to make it sound convincing.

> *My last project was a romantic comedy in the $300,000 range.*
> **Translation:** My friend's wedding video cost me about $30 in videotapes.

10. No matter how bad your first video project may be, enter it in every film and television festival that requires no entry fee. If you enter enough of them, you will start winning awards.

> *The video I just produced won the Golden Nugget award at the Moose Jaw Outdoorsmen Film Festival.*
> After your win, be sure to list on your bio that you are an 'award-winning filmmaker.'

Seems easy, doesn't it? Keep this list in full view and follow these rules religiously. Just remember, when you become famous to act difficult and don't return phone calls, you're sure to be a hit.

Chapter Seven

Case Studies

Inspiring Stories—
A Dose of Reality

The first part of this book dealt with the information you need to know in order to produce your own successful television productions. This chapter deals with real life scenarios on how producers put their projects together and made them a reality. Each project was chosen because of its unique funding structure. The case studies range from small to large budgets and deal with all areas of the television industry from documentaries to dramas. Stories like these are the inspiration that allows the rest of us to trudge forward with the program ideas that we so desperately believe in.

Through ups and downs, the producers interviewed got their projects off the ground. There are many stories about producers who were tenacious and refused to give up. You will notice that this is the common thread in the stories you are about to read. Even though their projects are different, the ability to never give up always shines through.

When I worked with new producers and was faced with dealing with many proposals, I could always tell which producers were going to finish their projects. You could see in them the determination to realize their projects no matter what the cost. I'm sure that after reading these stories you too will feel inspired to move ahead with your project.

Always remember to inject yourself with a healthy dose of reality because there will be pitfalls ahead. Learn from the following producers' success stories in order to achieve your own.

Mira Niagolova–Mira Productions
Trafficking Cinderella—One-Hour Documentary

I'm from Bulgaria and I'm fairly new to Canada. In Bulgaria I worked for Bulgarian National Television where I was employed in many different areas of the film and television industry. I was a producer, editor, script writer, anchor, and programmer. Essentially, I wore many different hats and performed several different duties. Then I emigrated to Canada with my husband several years ago when he was offered a job.

After attending university to complete a degree, I found a job with the National Film Board working in international sales. My area of specialty is eastern Europe and it was on one of my trips to Prague that I got the idea for my documentary *Trafficking Cinderella*. The idea came to me out of the blue and it was on a subject I never thought I would be interested in.

One evening as a friend and I were walking down the street, he showed me a girl he said was a prostitute. I was very surprised because she didn't look like a prostitute. She was very pretty and looked like she was waiting for a friend or relative, not for a client. There was something in her posture that captivated me, it was as if she was tough and resilient yet vulnerable at the same time. It was the way she held her hands, as if protecting herself. I returned to Canada but I could not forget this girl, her image didn't leave me in peace. Her image compelled me to begin researching the problem of prostitution in Eastern Europe.

After researching the subject for a while, I decided that this was a documentary I wanted to make. It was a time when I knew I had enough experience to produce my own programs and felt that this was a project with some significance—it had meaning. I decided to begin producing it, but first I had to find money.

It was tough to find financing and there were times when there didn't seem to be any glimmer of hope. I first contacted a broadcaster to try and obtain a broadcast license. The broadcaster I called told me that they would get back to me in a few months which seemed too long to wait, plus I was scared of being rejected, so I didn't bother. Next I applied to an arts council for a grant for projects from first-time producers and I was rejected. I considered applying to Telefilm Canada, but the process seemed so complicated to a newcomer like myself that I didn't apply. Every other place I contacted told me I had to have a broadcast license in order to apply for financing, but the broadcasters were so overwhelmed by proposals that it was going to be months before I heard back from them. It was a Catch-22 situation. I began to feel as if I had to unlock a door but I didn't have a key.

I told a friend of mine about the project and as she worked for a development bank, she was able to give me a small grant. I started to look for a crew and was able to find a very good cinematographer who was willing to defer his fee. Even with the grant and his deferral, I still didn't have enough money to begin production. It was at this point that I found an executive producer who loved my idea and agreed to help me attract broadcasters and money from Telefilm Canada. Once we began to work out the details, I realized that taking on an executive producer would cause the budget to rise significantly and that this producer would have a great deal of control over the project, something I wasn't comfortable with. After some soul searching, I decided to continue on my own.

I agonized over whether or not I was doing the right thing. I was scared that I was jeopardizing the project and that I was ruining my chances of ever getting the project off the ground. I couldn't sleep so I called my cinematographer who told me "If you're going to swim, you have to jump first," so I decided to finish the project myself and keep the project small to maintain the vision I first had.

It was with the incredibly small grant from my friend that I started to film my documentary. We made our first trip to Europe and filmed some very good interviews but we needed money to go back and continue filming. Thankfully, I received two travel grants from the Canadian government that paid for our return trips but this didn't improve my long-term money situation. I then applied to the Soros Documentary Fund, a documentary fund based in the United States. I waited a long time to hear about my application and just when I needed the money the most, I received a grant from them which helped to pay for the rest of the filming.

We shot all of the interviews we needed in Europe and now I had to begin thinking about the editing process and how I was going to pay for it. Of course, I didn't have much money but because of wise budgeting during filming, I still had some money left over from the Soros Documentary Fund.

I talked to the manager of an editing facility who agreed to give me a fifty percent discount on editing costs. This allowed me to edit thirty-five minutes of the program. At this point, I decided to try and approach a broadcaster and asked the Women's Television Network (WTN) if they might be interested. After looking at the footage they agreed to give me a national broadcast license which in turn helped me to complete the editing on the documentary. It's ironic because it seems like every time I really needed the money, I was able to find it.

I found that on one hand it is very complicated and frustrating to find funding for projects in

Canada, but on the other hand I met great people who helped me tremendously. It seemed to me that when people could see that I was sincere in my conviction, that this was a good project and that I was going to complete it at all costs, my enthusiasm became contagious and they helped me in any way they could.

I think that if you really believe in a project, somewhere in the end it will pay off. It's not a rational process; once you decide to start a project, even if you don't have the money, you just begin. It's like having a baby. When you decide to have a baby you want it now, you don't want to wait nine months. I believe that you shouldn't start any project unless you believe in it one hundred percent; this is what helped keep me going through the times when I didn't have any money and it looked like everything was going to fall apart. Even though it was exhausting having no money, if I had to do it all over again I would do it exactly the same way.

The documentary is now finished and I have applied for another grant which I'm hoping to receive so I can pay myself and my bills, giving this *Cinderella* story a happy ending.

Joan Prowse--Cinefocus Canada
Beauty and the Beach–One-Hour Documentary

I began making documentaries after graduating from university with a degree in radio &

television. I started making political documentaries on Canadian issues in partnership with my husband John. We made videos on our own time as we were both working during the day at paying jobs. From there we branched out into making corporate videos for clients in the health care and non-profit fields.

We began making our documentaries with a very small crew and very little money. It was myself, John, John's brother Carl, and their friend Dave as the production team. It was great working with them because they were able to obtain equipment and facilities for next to nothing. I find it hard to bargain for cheap prices but I would get on the phone and beg, borrow and steal to make these projects happen. Essentially, I would be upfront with the people I was dealing with and explain that my budget was low but that I had a dream and I intended to carry it through. I believe that if people can catch your spirit and conviction and are able to see that you believe in what you are doing, they will help. My philosophy is that everyone in this industry has been helped by someone at one point in time and if you catch them at the right moment, they will be inclined to help you as well.

After making several more political documentaries and industrial videos for clients, we were making enough money that I was able to quit my day job and focus on our projects full-time. I realized that it was time to take off the training wheels and let go of the security blanket of a full-time job. So I jumped right in.

We decided that we would still make industrial videos, but we wanted to slowly begin work on our own broadcast projects. This was the second stage of growth for our company. We needed to be less dependent on our clients and more reliant on ourselves. We realized that we wanted to focus on broadcast-oriented projects that could capture a large audience and that the projects we were making about Canadian political stories were not going to achieve this goal.

You have to think internationally if you want your projects to go beyond Canada. I decided to open up my mind and think of an idea that would travel well. It was around this time that I started helping my sister at her bathing suit store. It was Christmas and she needed the help while I needed the extra money. It seemed lame that I had quit my job and started my own company yet here I was working as a clerk in a bathing suit store. I decided to turn this situation to my advantage. I believe that people need to open up their closed minds. Some people think that they are in a horrible situation, working at a job they don't like, when in fact a potential opportunity may exist. You just have to recognize the opportunity and grasp it.

While I was working at the store, I began to wonder why it was taking so long for women to buy a bathing suit. Some of them would be in the changing room for two hours trying on suits and would then ask their husband's opinions. The men loved the suits but the women would hem and haw because they felt that they didn't look attractive. While the men were waiting, they would pick out bathing suits for themselves and pay for them without trying them on. I realized that when it comes to body image, the difference between the sexes is interesting.

I saw that women's views of themselves in a bathing suit was a problem of self-consciousness and I decided to get to the root of the problem by researching the history of women's bathing suits. It was then that I decided to make a documentary that examined the problem women had with bathing suits and self-image and to explore this issue in a larger historical context.

After I finished my initial research I began searching for development funds that would help to fund further research. It was hard to find the money. One thing I learned right away is that you have to see opportunity in everything you do. Every book you read, every person you meet might be able to help you to advance your goal. Luckily, I was able to get development money from the Ontario Film Development Corporation and the Ontario Heritage Foundation just before they ceased giving out research and development funds for film and video projects.

I then started calling women's organizations and federal and provincial governments for research purposes and I was never too proud to ask if they might be interested in funding the project or if they knew of anyone who would. I made sure that I had a proposal ready whenever

I called an organization so that if they were interested I was able to send them a proposal right away. When I pinpointed an organization I called ahead to find out to whom I should send the proposal and then made a point of talking to that person directly. This was ultimately a very depressing exercise because it didn't bring any funding to the project.

It was time to try another tactic. Thankfully, my sister came up with the idea that if I couldn't raise money by applying for it, I should be proactive and find the money myself. She suggested that I hold a fashion show to raise funds and said that she would gladly help assemble the bathing suits. The next thing I knew we were spending months putting together this fashion show extravaganza. It wasn't a tiny fashion show; we had video presentations highlighting key events of the century and we had designers interpret their vision of bathing suits from different eras. I was able to get the models for free and swim wear companies loaned me period bathing suits for the show.

The fashion show paid off in an unexpected way. The media picked up the story and wrote articles and published photos of the models in the swim wear. I was interviewed on television and radio. The fashion show ended up being a big promotional blitz even though this wasn't my original intention. However, while the fashion show was successful in generating media coverage, it was not successful at raising funds. I had to try something else.

This was when I came up with the idea of a promotional postcard. The front of the postcard featured my two associate producers and I in our bathing suits, in the middle of winter, with the caption "Our funds are frozen!" Then I went to the library and got a list of all the swim wear manufacturers, sunglass companies, suntan lotion manufacturers, and basically any company that had anything to do with the beach or swimming, and sent them one of my postcards.

While I was sending them out I was also preparing for the first day of filming. I was prepared to go ahead even if we didn't have all the money because I believe that there will never be enough money. I know that ideas can go stale and if you shelve a project you will eventually drift back into everyday life and the project will never get made.

The postcards turned out to be a success and four swim wear companies donated money and supplies. The only faux pas I made happened when one company asked how much money I was looking for and I gave them an overly-ambitious amount which they declined. Next time I'll ask "How much do you normally give to a project of this sort?"

At the same time, I began approaching television broadcasters. It was very difficult and I kept getting rejected. Luckily, I began to get interest from educational broadcasters who were willing to become second-window broadcasters. The Saskatchewan Communications Network (SCN) in Saskatchewan came on board as did the Knowledge Network in British Columbia.

What I really needed now was a national broadcaster. In the beginning I had approached the Women's Television Network (WTN) and had been turned down because my documentary was a single program and they were only interested in funding series. However, they liked the idea, felt bad saying no and suggested that if I wanted to change the situation I could write to WTN's vice president of programming. I wrote a letter and the next thing I knew I received a call from WTN saying that they would give me a national broadcast license.

During this time, John had been calling CFCF Television in Montreal, trying to interest them in another project we were developing. When they turned him down he pitched them the bathing suit idea and to his surprise they agreed to give us a second window license. This was a good learning experience—if someone says no to your project, pitch them one of your other ideas.

John came to the rescue again by suggesting that I call broadcasters in Alberta, his home province. It worked, and CFCN in Calgary and CFRN in Edmonton came on board as further second-window broadcasters.

Now that I had accumulated enough license fees, I was able to apply to the Cable Television Fund for fifteen percent of the budget. I also applied to the Canadian Independent Film and Video Fund and was awarded a production grant.

What I found was that once things started to roll, and people found out about our project, funds began to fall into place. You have to get over that initial difficult fundraising hurdle and once you do, it gets easier.

While continuing to raise funds, I began to shoot the documentary. Because money from funding agencies does not all come at once, and I had bills to pay from the start of production, I had to get a loan from the bank to help bridge my financing. Thankfully, I had a good relationship with my bank manager and this helped to ease the process of obtaining a loan. I also received some unexpected help from my mother-in-law who normally donates money to cultural groups and decided to give us a donation. When my own mother heard about my mother-in-law's generosity, not one to be outdone, she donated funds as well.

By this time, the filming of the documentary was complete and it was time to begin editing. Unfortunately we didn't have enough funds to pay for post-production work. We decided to approach the post-production facility where we had previously edited our clients' videos and to ask them if they would be willing to give us a deal. As we had a good relationship with them, they agreed to give us a fifty percent discount on the editing costs.

We then began editing the documentary and when it was in rough-cut stage, I showed it to CBC Newsworld. I had originally approached the CBC months before and they had turned me down but had encouraged me to come back when I had footage to show them. This time they decided to accept the program and became my second national broadcaster. Access Alberta, the educational broadcaster in Alberta, also came on board at this stage and I acquired another second-window broadcaster.

We finally completed the documentary but we still found that we had bills to pay. I sent a copy of the program to French-language broadcaster Radio-Canada, who gave me a license for the French market and I was able to secure funds from Telefilm Canada which enabled me to translate the program into French. I also applied for the Ontario tax credit and the Federal tax credit which took over a year to receive. Lastly, I have found a great distributor who has sold my documentary to the Learning Channel in the United States and to other broadcasters in Europe and Asia.

In total, it took me two and a half years to complete this project plus raise the financing. You must remember, this was not a big-budget documentary. I believe that we succeeded because we were tenacious. You have to be prepared to receive a lot of negative response, but you can't let that stop you. Always be ready for rejection and ready to pitch one of your other projects. Turn the negative responses to your advantage.

To date, I have not made a lot of money from the project but I have been able to pay all my bills. I have to say that I learned a lot from the experience and I believe that there's value in learning. The project raised awareness of our company among television broadcasters so now when I call, they know my name. There are going to be times when you're starting out when you don't make money, but you don't go broke, and your program is shown in film festivals and by broadcasters around the world. This to me is success.

Sandra Kennerson—Kennerson Productions
Canadian Adventure Guide —Lifestyle Series

I became a producer through circumstance. I had just finished college with a diploma in corporate communications and I was working in my field plus modeling to make extra money. One day, my modeling agency sent me on assignment to a television series that needed models. I had been working on-set for a few days when I got to talking to the owner of the production company. He startled me by saying that I shouldn't be in corporate communications but in sales. He said that he saw a quality in me that would make a good salesperson. I began to think about his advice and soon found an opening for a sales representative at a television production company. They needed salespeople who could find sponsors for their lifestyle series. I didn't know anything about sales but I somehow bullied my way into the position.

I observed how the other salespeople approached potential sponsors and I had to learn quickly how to make cold calls by targeting companies who I thought would be interested in participating in our programs. After targeting the companies, I would call and request further information about their products and services.

Once I felt I could speak knowledgeably about their business and products, I would call and ask to speak to the marketing director. I would tell them about our series and why we felt that they would be an excellent sponsor. Then I would request a meeting to discuss it further.

If the meeting was successful, we would negotiate their involvement in the form of either a cash contribution or a barter deal. Barter is a method whereby the sponsor donates goods or services in return for a promotional credit on the series. At the time we were producing a home build-it series and sponsors donated materials such as lumber, or would arrange for their experts to help us build the homes.

After I had arranged sponsorship for the series, the producer unexpectedly quit so I walked in and asked for the job. The production executives balked at the idea because I had no experience but I was persuasive enough to convince them to try me out for a week.

I was terrified when I walked on-set the first day but I explained to the crew that I was their new producer and as they were the experts in their area, they should continue to handle their jobs as before. I would be the one to harness all the activity and be responsible for making sure that the sponsors and broadcasters were kept happy. The series ended up becoming a dynamic team effort. We completed it under budget and ahead of schedule.

Out of this series came several other series that I produced for the company. Eventually I decided to take my knowledge and expertise in television in a different direction. I had started to develop a personal interest in adventure activities and I felt a series about outdoor adventure activities would be welcomed by Canadian viewers. I knew there was an opportunity to provide a series that was currently missing from television so I came up with the idea for the *Canadian Adventure Guide*. It would be a series that would demonstrate to the audience what adventure activities were available but it would be constructed in such a way that the armchair enthusiast, as well as the adventure enthusiast, could enjoy.

I first proposed the idea to the production company I was working for but they weren't interested. I then explained the idea to someone who was a mentor of mine. They told me that this was such a winning idea that if I didn't do it, there were other producers who would. They also gave me advice that has always worked for me; if your passion is involved in this idea, let your passion drive you for there will be many times when you are starting out that people will say "no" and close doors, but you can't let that stop you. You have to be persistent. My mentor was right, because getting the series going wasn't as hard as I thought it would be.

The first step in producing this series was to quit my job and start my own company. I then began working full-time on the idea. To start off, I knew that I had the experience to produce a series, and I knew that I could find sponsors. The only experience I didn't have was dealing with broadcasters, so this was to be my first challenge.

Before approaching broadcasters, I decided to do some research. I considered that I had three audiences; the viewers, the broadcasters and the sponsors. So I knew I first had to find what the demographics of the viewing audience for the series would be, then I needed to find the right broadcaster and the right sponsor.

Once I had conducted my research on the audience statistics, I had to find a broadcaster. It terrified me to deal with them but I had to get over this intimidation and began by sending three broadcasters a proposal. I also produced a demo tape to go along with the proposal for the series. The demo tape wasn't necessarily slick or expensive-looking as I didn't have any money, but it gave a brief example of what one episode would look like. I was concerned that since I was new, broadcasters might question my experience. I made sure to note on my proposal who my production partners were, such as the post-house I would be dealing with, my composer, and the people who would be recording the audio for the series. They were all well-established companies and individuals and I believe that this added credibility to my proposal.

The first two broadcasters I approached turned me down but the third, the Life Network, was very interested. We worked out a barter deal whereby they didn't have to pay me a license fee but I was able to sell some of the commercial time contained within the series to sponsors.

Once I made this deal, it was matter of finding sponsors who would be interested in the series. I pinpointed the sponsors who I wanted to attract and set up meetings with them. I arranged six meetings with six sponsors and was able to make deals with three of them. One of the main sponsors I was hoping to get was Chevrolet and I was lucky to get their approval at our first meeting. The other two sponsors were the North Face, an adventure equipment company, and Salomon, a ski manufacturer.

The funding literally came together in eight weeks. As Chevrolet was our main sponsor, we called the series *Chevrolet Canadian Adventure Guide*. Having Chevrolet's name in the title was originally approved by the broadcaster but as the series progressed they became uneasy with the situation. They felt that having Chevrolet's name in the title implied infomercial programming.

I am careful not to confuse these two issues. There must be a clear delineation between editorial comment and the views of the sponsor. Viewers are a very educated and astute audience. If they feel that they're being hit over the head with a commercial message then they will change the channel.

I am very careful with how I handle sponsorship in my series. I have learned from past experience that programs cannot look like commercial messages. There is a fine line when dealing with a sponsor's products during a program. On one hand you have to give the sponsor what they perceive is fair value for their money but on the other hand you can't let them dictate the editorial content of your program. You have to be sensitive to what the viewer will accept. Sponsors are also aware of this fine line and are careful not to deal with a program that looks like an infomercial.

In the future, I hope that broadcasters will change their attitude towards sponsored programming. Broadcasters should allow producers to bring money-raising opportunities to the table. Currently broadcasters say "sponsorship" as if it's a dirty word although it's ironic that more and more broadcasters are looking for sponsors for their own in-house productions.

The hardest thing about attracting corporate sponsors is making them see the value of participating in your series. It's all about audience statistics and demographics. Sponsors want to make sure that they are reaching the people who would potentially buy their products and must be certain that this is the audience your series will be attract. Sponsors also want to be sure that their product will be featured in the body of the program as this reinforces their involvement.

It's the commercial time, combined with coverage in the body of the program, that makes it an attractive package for sponsors. I generally give sponsors three production elements; a prominent mention in the opening and closing credits, and a sponsored element in the body of the program.

When I first started approaching sponsors, it was by trial and error. I made mistakes, but I learned from them. The important rule is to always be well-prepared for meetings. I do my research in advance by finding out everything I can about the potential client. I make about six phone calls to the company in advance asking for information and only on the seventh phone call do I actually speak to the marketing director and request a meeting. Before I go into that meeting, I know their products inside and out.

Producers need to use this same principle when approaching broadcasters. Do not waste a broadcaster's time by sending them a proposal that doesn't suit their network. I speak to a lot of new producers who send their proposals to every network. This is the wrong approach

because all broadcasters have different mandates. You can't take a shotgun approach when
going after sponsors or broadcasters.

Getting a broadcaster is a real challenge, and
is the first step towards turning your series or
program idea into reality. The tricky part to
dealing with broadcasters over sponsored
programming is the fact that the broadcaster
wants to be certain that you are going to have
money from sponsors before they sign on, but
sponsors won't come on board until you have a
broadcaster. It's the chicken and egg story. It's a
real juggling act. But what I've learned is that if
one door closes, another opens. If a sponsor or a
broadcaster say "no," there will be others to take
their place.

As for the *Canadian Adventure Guide*, with the
financing from our three sponsors I was able to
produce the series on a very tight budget. I was
able to accomplish it on a tight budget because
everyone I was working with believed in the
series and knew I didn't have much money.
Luckily, the post-production facility where we
were going to be editing agreed to give me a
discount price if I was willing to edit during off-
hours on evenings and weekends. This is a good
way to save money on post-production; make a
deal with your post house to edit during slow
times such as the midnight-to-6:00AM shift.

Because of all this cost saving, I was able to
produce the series on a shoestring budget and
the series aired on the Life Network. After the

first season on the Life Network, I switched the series to the Outdoor Life Network for the broadcast of the second season. This time I received a license fee from the broadcaster and I was also able to sell some of the commercial time to my sponsors. Unfortunately, Chevrolet was no longer able to participate so the title was transformed to the *Canadian Adventure Guide*. I am now working on the third season of the series and the success of it has led to my creating another series with the same sponsors for another network.

Surprisingly, I have never found approaching sponsors as difficult as I originally perceived it to be. A lot of times people imagine things to be more difficult than they actually are. If you can pick up the phone, call a sponsor, and speak intelligently about your series, it all comes together smoothly. I don't want to make it sound so easy that all you have to do is pick up the phone, because nothing is ever that easy, but don't let being afraid stop you.

One of the biggest frustrations in dealing with sponsors is getting them to return your phone calls. I once had a sponsor with whom I had been trying to get in touch with for over a year. I kept leaving messages on his answering machine for him to contact me. I finally realized that I had been calling this gentlemen for a year and decided to get creative by leaving a message saying "I just wanted to call and say 'happy anniversary' as you have now been avoiding my calls for a year." The message was left in good humour and it worked because he called me back ten minutes later. I never did sign him on but I finally got to talk to him. This is how persistence pays off.

A word of advice for new producers who are thinking about approaching sponsors; never make "maybe" phone calls. By this I mean make sure that you have a broadcaster lined up before you approach sponsors because you cannot call sponsors and say "maybe" a certain broadcaster is going to broadcast the series. You cannot test the waters. You have to be certain that the broadcaster is set before you call the sponsor because you can't risk losing them. If you're asking a sponsor to invest in your series, you have to exude confidence and make them believe in your show to the point where there is no question about your ability to produce a quality series.

For my series I always try to get a title sponsor, meaning a main sponsor. Car manufacturers are my choice for title sponsors. Then I find two supporting sponsors. Their combined funds make up the budget for the series. Even with all of their money, we still operate on a shoestring budget, but you can't have the series look like it was made on such a low budget, you have to make it look high-quality.

I am fortunate to have an excellent track record with broadcasters and sponsors. One of the sponsors, who has been with me since the beginning, has already called and said that they have placed me in their marketing plans for next year even though I haven't asked them for money. It's a great feeling to be given money without asking for it.

I believe that producers need to do a lot of advance research and know who their potential audiences are for their series. You have to keep in mind that broadcasters are interested in programs that audiences are going to watch as well as in programs that are going to attract advertisers. Broadcasters make a good chunk of their money selling commercial time during programming and are looking for program ideas that will sell to advertisers.

You need to make things as easy as possible for the broadcaster. You must remember that on a typical day, they are being bombarded by producers as well as trying to complete their daily workload. As producers, we often feel that we are the only people whom the broadcaster needs to deal with but the reality is that they have to deal with hundreds of producers. Don't be put off if a broadcaster isn't returning your phone calls and doesn't want to meet with you. Instead, mail in your proposal as everything is done via paper. Remember, the number of producers is mushrooming every day and broadcasters have to bear the weight. Don't take their non-response personally, it's just the nature of the business.

I cannot stress how important it is for new producers to be persistent. Never take "no" for an answer. If the people you are approaching turn you down, work to turn that rejection into an acceptance.   I think that when you are passionate about a program and it is well researched, well prepared, and well presented, you will make it happen. Just remember, there are no limits to what you can achieve.

Arnie Gelbart – Gala Films
The Worst Witch —Children's Series

My original intention was not to become a producer, but an architect, as I had studied architecture in Montreal. Somewhere along the way I became interested in film and began working in the film industry. I was then able to combine my two loves by making short films about architecture. Eventually, I began working on topics other than architecture and proceeded to direct and work on feature films and television projects.

When I felt I had enough knowledge about the business end of the industry, I started my own production company. I produced projects for television such as documentaries and continued to work on feature films. At that time, documentaries were the mainstay of my business and even now I keep a close relationship with the documentary genre.

At the outset, I didn't find it difficult to produce projects for my own company. From experience, I knew how to make projects happen. Initially, the documentaries I produced were small but grew more ambitious when I began producing long-format documentaries for the CBC and other broadcasters. From there I moved into producing documentary series and multiple-episode documentaries. I find that there is a natural progression that takes over once you gain experience in producing. After you have gained sufficient knowledge, your projects become more ambitious just as mine did.

After producing several documentary series, I began producing feature films. My first feature was *Lilies* and I have produced many since such as the critically acclaimed *Hanging Garden*. Some of these films were done in collaboration with other production companies in Quebec or other provinces.

Luckily, there are many incentives to producing in Quebec and the province really supports its filmmakers with tax incentives and government funds. Fundraising was never as hard as I thought it would be. Of course, it's gotten more difficult now with cutbacks and I, along with every other producer, am forced to look for funding abroad. This is how *The Worst Witch* was produced, as a co-production with Britain.

The series idea started with a friend of mine who was a producer in Britain. He had acquired the rights to a series of children's books about a modern-day witch interacting with a group of pre-teens.   The books had enjoyed a large following in Britain and he felt that they would make an excellent television series.   He mentioned the idea to me and I immediately felt that this was a series I wanted to be involved with.

Our first step was to find broadcasters on both sides of the Atlantic.   I was able to bring YTV on board for the national English-language market and, as the series was going to be versioned into the French language, I was able to sign TFO and Radio-Canada for the French-language market.   In Britain, my co-producer was able to find ITV, a well-known British commercial network and he was able to attract United, a large British producer as a third partner.

Once we found broadcasters, we went after other forms of financing.   For my efforts, we received financing from Telefilm Canada as well as tax credits.   Because a portion of the series was shot in Quebec, we were able to access the Quebec tax credit as well as the Federal tax credit.

My British co-producer was able to find a distributor who agreed to advance funds in anticipation of future sales in the form of a distribution advance.   Revenue from sales on distribution are shared between myself and my British co-producer.

We broke the production of the series into sections.   Approximately twenty percent of the series was shot in Canada, and the rest in Britain, but all the post-production was completed in

Canada. We had two directors, one Canadian and the other British, our writers were from both countries, and our actors were a combination of Canadian and British talent.

All in all, it was a smooth-running production. Of course, there is always a lot of paperwork and bureaucracy involved when making international co-productions but it wasn't as hard as I had originally thought it would be. I didn't really know what I was getting into in terms of paperwork so I just barreled ahead and began to fill out the papers. Once you put the wheels in motion you will find paperwork is not the onerous task you once imagined. If you want to be a producer you have to understand that dealing with paperwork is going to take up a gigantic amount of your time and if you're faced with producing many pro-jects, you have to keep on top of the paperwork. Handling the administrative end of producing is a large part of a producer's job, especially when dealing with international co-productions.

I now produce quite a few international co-productions with documentary projects leading the forefront. Generally, I find my co-production partners by attending foreign television markets and festivals and establishing relationships with producers who have similar programming interests. The idea is to find subjects that are of interest to both parties.

Sometimes I pitch my idea to them and if they're interested we pursue it further and other times they pitch their idea to me. It's a give-and-take situation. We determine what idea would be best suited in the marketplace and then proceed with that idea. It's very important to be aware of what broadcasters are looking for both in Canada and abroad. Producers need to read industry newspapers and magazines to keep abreast of broadcaster's needs. Even reading the TV guide is an important task. Be aware of what broadcasters at home are airing by reading your local TV guide and follow European broadcast schedules by subscribing to international TV guides or checking out the internet.

If you want to produce a large series, the reality is that you have to find an international co-production partner. Even the Americans can no longer afford to carry large budgets themselves. They too are forced to find co-production dollars.

Keep in mind that no matter how far abroad you look for financing, your home base is going to be the first place you must look. This is especially true when dealing with broadcasters. When you manage to interest a foreign broadcaster, the first thing they are going to ask is "Who is your Canadian broadcaster?" If your answer is "Nobody," then they are going to wonder why they should be interested when no Canadian broadcaster is. In the case of *The Worst Witch*, it was fortuitous that the British producer and I had been friends and knew that we could work together. We both had track records in our respective countries, so this made finding broadcasters easier.

You may run into situations where the Canadian broadcaster won't put up money until they know who the foreign broadcasters are but these situations are only created when the broadcaster is not really interested in the project. Generally, the Canadian broadcaster will say that they are interested but will only agree to put up a certain amount of the budget. It's up to you to make up the difference through foreign pre-sales.

As a producer, if you are thinking of making large projects and co-productions, I recommend that you love what you are doing because if you don't, you're going to hate it later as the majority of work is not going to be easy. You have to have an all-consuming passion for your project to drive you during those difficult times. You also have to make sure that you are constantly working on new ideas to carry you when you are waiting for projects you have developed to come through.

Our co-production on *The Worst Witch* has been very successful in Canada and in Britain, where it has done very well in the ratings. Our first series of thirteen episodes has been so successful that our broadcasters and investors have agreed to fund another series of thirteen episodes.

A majority of this success is due to my great relationship with my British co-production partner. We were lucky to be friends first, then business partners. We knew each other and trusted each other. Trust and forming relation-

ships are very important points to being successful in the entertainment industry. The best way
to ensure this trust is to find the right partner,
and the right subject.

Laszlo Barna – Barna Alper Productions
DaVinci's Inquest —Dramatic Series

When I started out in television I was a
director, not a producer. That soon changed
when I became discouraged watching the
producers who hired me not be able to raise
money for a project, the result being that I was
expected to direct a program with no money. I
thought "Surely to God, this could be done more
efficiently." So I started out slowly as a
producer, initially raising money for my own
small projects. Funnily enough, at the time I
didn't know what a producer did, I only knew I
didn't like them. I realized that producing was
not that far above directing as it involves putting
together talented people with the right amount
of financing.

I learned producing on the job and acquired
fundraising abilities by applying to different
funding agencies. Because of the peculiarities of
Canadian television funding, you learn
fundraising by filling out applications and you
eventually become an expert at it.

I formed a partnership with a colleague of
mine and the first project we produced that was

important in terms of getting to know broadcasters was a series called *Work Week* for TVOntario and CBC Newsworld. It was a very difficult time for independent producers because television programming was produced in-house by broadcasters, who were buying very little from independent producers. When more cable channels were introduced, a whole new world opened up for independent producers. The growth of our company changed dramatically with the emergence of the cable channels. If CBC Newsworld hadn't been licensed, we would have had a very hard time starting out. Broadcasters have now done a complete turnaround; instead of producing their own productions, they are out sourcing programming to independent producers.

It took over a year to put together the financing for *Work Week*. Even though we already had TVOntario and Newsworld, I had to raise outside financing as well as find other broadcasters who could contribute to the budget. We finally raised all of the budget and made 104 episodes over four years. This was our entry to dealing with broadcasters and it made me realize how broadcasters see the world and what their needs are. They are basically looking for producers who can, with limited resources, fill a time slot with quality programming and deliver on time.

In my opinion, producing is rather simple if you realize that ideas rule. By this I mean that you have to come up with a good idea and start to ask yourself questions about the idea.

For example, is it marketable? Who are the creative talents going to be, and so on. Eventually, you start gravitating toward the right answers as opposed to the wrong ones and you rationalize whether or not this idea is going to fly.

After *Work Week*, we began producing documentary series for various networks. We also became fledgling producers of drama as we produced two movies-of-the-week for the CBC. We decided to concentrate on series production because broadcasters are primarily looking for a series product. As a company, we also found it easier to grow while working on a series because we knew that we had long-term work instead of constantly having to audition for our next gig.

By the time we started producing *DaVinci's Inquest*, our first dramatic series, we were seasoned producers. The idea for a series about a Vancouver coroner solving crimes came from a long time friend of mine, Chris Haddock. He is a writer and had worked in television for several years. He told me that he had this great idea for a series, but he was always coming up with great ideas and then never committing them to paper. I told him that if he would write it down, I would personally walk it over to the CBC. This time he surprised me and wrote a few pages, making the idea well formed. I did walk it over to the CBC and they liked the idea. As we had produced other dramatic works for them, they had confidence in our ability to produce and felt that Chris had a lot of experience as a writer.

Of course, it wasn't so simple that the CBC said "Yes" and put the series on-air. They first provided us with development money to write three scripts and then we had to deal with a lot of administrative details. Once we provided the scripts, they gave us a list of things to change. We re-drafted the scripts only to have more requested changes. Finally, on the basis of three final scripts, they ordered the series for broadcast and gave us a national license fee.

We then had to find the rest of the financing for the series by obtaining a distribution partner and applying to funding agencies. The budget was finally made up of money from the CBC, a distributor, Telefilm Canada, the Canadian Television Fund and Ontario and Federal tax credits. Because the series was shot in British Columbia, we were also able to access funds from British Columbia Film and the BC tax credit. In total, it was about a year and a half from the first time we proposed the series to the CBC until the time when we had secured financing and were able to begin production.

By industry standards this was a quick turn-around. We were able to get a quick turnaround because the scripts were so good. After the series aired everyone was very happy with the outcome, so the CBC has ordered another season and all of our original financing partners are back in place.

The hardest thing for me to deal with as a producer is the administrative details that come along with producing, especially the paperwork and bureaucracy involved in fundraising. Our projects might have at least seven different sources of financing and we have to keep up with all the paperwork that goes along with the contracts. To deal with this, you need an infrastructure in order to be able to service your funding partners. The other thing that is hard is the fact that money you are entitled to receive is not always there when you need it, making it very difficult to do your job properly.

Because a lot of the traditional subsidy funding is collapsing, it has become harder to find financing in Canada so you often have to look offshore for financial partners and broadcasters. This then compromises the level of Canadian content in the project. Even though we had a lot of fundraising hassles with *DaVinci's Inquest*, we led somewhat of a charmed life because the scripts were so good. Contrary to what people may think, there is no "fix" preventing new producers from breaking through. We had never done a dramatic series before but the weight of the scripts and the production team was what tipped the balance in our favour. Surprisingly, it is not as much of a hassle breaking through as one would think.

Projects are often turned down by broadcasters and this has happened to me, but there was some justice to it because the ideas weren't as good as they could have been. I was sort of glad that the broadcasters took a pass on those ideas because if your idea isn't ready to go to air, you need someone to tell you or else you will barrel ahead. The truth is, some projects are worthwhile, and others aren't.

The industry is very competitive but remember, the dice haven't been thrown so if you're persistent, and you have good talent behind you, then you will get there. If you are consistently being turned down, then you have to look at your idea or the way you sell the idea to see if it's worthwhile. It's more important to be self-critical than to be critical about the system itself. Oddly enough, I find the Canadian television industry to be one of the most democratic of industries.   I have never seen a television executive be comfortable with turning down a project. They never know where the next good idea is coming from or where the next brilliant project lies.

I used to waste a lot of time worrying about calling up a big shot only to find out later that worrying is a total waste of time.   Don't be fearful. Big shots will talk to you because their well-being depends on finding the next critical hit and you may have it. If broadcasters turn you down the first three times, make sure you go back the fourth time. By this time, you are no longer auditioning. They know who you are and will listen carefully. If you are turned down the fourth time, you have to realize that you either have a rotten idea or you are approaching the wrong broadcaster.

Be certain that you are approaching the right broadcaster. There are a lot of people who never understand the notion of targeting an idea properly. They never stop seeing the world from their own little window and will continue to try and sell their ideas to broadcasters who are not interested.

You must also realize that if you're going into producing thinking that you are going to make a lot of money, then you are in it for the wrong reasons. Sometimes you can pay your bills, but it's hard to make a profit. Producers always say that distributors make all the money, distributors say that banks make all the money, and banks say that shareholders make all the money, so in the end it turns out that two guys you don't even know have made all the money.

Despite funding drawbacks, I still believe that Canada is one of the most generous countries when it comes to subsidies for television. We live in a country where if you're young, you can get a headstart. Be brave and find out what makes your heart throb from an artistic point of view. As long as you are sure of who you are, you cannot be hurt.

Chapter Eight

Finance Reference Guide

This is the information most readers have been waiting for. For those who read the previous chapters, this section of the book is where you can find all those potential revenue sources we have been talking about. For the experienced producers who skipped the how-to section, this is the information that is going to make your lives a lot easier.

The following pages list places to find financing for television. This is information I began compiling when I realized there was no central resource book that listed all the places to find financing for Canadian television productions. This list is by no means exhaustive but is representative of the types of funding available for television.

Canadian National Television Broadcasters

The first section deals with the names and addresses of Canadian National Television Broadcasters. These are the broadcasters you have to interest first in your quest to make television programming. They are the defacto "gate-keepers." They are the important first step to realizing your dream. Because of their importance, they are listed in first order on the following pages. This list does not contain all the Canadian national broadcasters but rather a list of the national broadcasters who have been known in the past to buy programming from independent producers. There are other Canadian national broadcasters that have been left off this list because they generally broadcast their own in-house programming and do not buy in large volume from independent producers. By all means you are welcome to try broadcasters who have been left off the list and if you do, you're well on your way to conquering the hardest part of being a producer; selling a program idea to a broadcaster who doesn't want to buy.

Canadian Provincial Television Broadcasters are listed next in the guide. These are broadcasters who broadcast within provincial borders and are known to buy "second windows" for television programming. As with national broadcasters, not all provincial broadcasters are listed, only the ones who have been known to deal with independent producers.

Canadian Provincial Television Broadcasters

This section of the guide also lists provincial funding agencies such as arts councils and government funding as well as television industry funds that provide financing to producers in their host provinces. Also in the provincial funding section are the agencies who administer provincial tax credits.

Provincial Funding Agencies

The provincial information is arranged coast to coast across Canada beginning on the west coast with British Columbia through to the east coast, finally ending in the NorthWest Territories.

National Funding Bodies

National Funding Bodies appear next in the finance guide. These organizations are government funding agencies and television industry funds that finance television programming on a national level. Producers from across Canada have the opportunity to apply to these funds. These funds generally provide a large portion of the producer's budgets and should be seriously considered when deciding whom to approach for financing.

Interim Financing

Interim financing is listed next in the guide. These are the financial institutions who provide short-term loans to producers to help bridge the times when producers are waiting for contracted financing to come in but cash is in short supply. The interim financing organizations listed in the guide are institutions who have been in the entertainment money-lending field for quite some time and are well-established. Being well-established generally means they are interested in giving large loans to experienced producers. You are welcome to approach them for funds but for smaller loan amounts you may be better to approach your own local bank for a loan or line of credit.

Foreign and American Broadcasters

Foreign and American broadcasters are last in the finance guide. As advised previously, it is best for producers to look in their own backyard of Canada when looking for financing. Approach Canadian broadcasters first when looking for a broadcast license and only approach foreign and American broadcasters if you feel you have a hot program idea that will travel well. I say this in order to save you disappointment.   If you are a new producer and approach broadcasters outside Canada, the results can be very discouraging.

Foreign and American broadcasters are reluctant to deal with producers whom they have never met and live in a foreign country. Like Canadian broadcasters, they are obligated to buy a certain percentage of programming from producers in their own country and they are reluctant to risk money, and time, on a producer located half way around the world. It is easier for them to deal with local producers. If the broadcaster is interested in your idea, they will most likely tell you they will consider investing upon viewing a rough cut, or an initial edited version, rather than investing at the proposal stage. This cuts down the risk to their investment and they are able to gauge what the program looks like before investing.

They will also want to see there is involvement from a Canadian broadcaster as they often take the attitude "if a Canadian broadcaster isn't interested then why should we?". This is the chicken and egg syndrome appearing again. You cannot sell to a foreign broadcaster until you have Canadian broadcast involvement and sometimes the Canadians won't become involved until you have interest from a foreign broadcaster.

The best way to approach Foreign and American broadcasters is to meet them at television festivals and introduce yourself. Follow up on the introduction with occasional correspondence so they are familiar with your name and then approach them with a program idea. It is a slow process but one that will pay off in the end.

Check the Facts

Check the Websites

Before you contact any of the organizations listed in the guide, it is imperative you call in advance to double check the address information is current and to confirm they are accepting proposals. Or better yet, check the websites listed to confirm the addresses. Remember businesses frequently change addresses.

Even though I have made every effort to be as up to date as possible, priorities change with broadcasters and funding bodies change funding criteria like the wind. It's up to you to do your homework and research current priorities with funding bodies and broadcasters.

Budget Cuts
Affect Funding

Be aware that funding bodies sometimes fold when their government backing is no longer available. Budget cuts hit everyone and often funding for the arts is the first to go. Check these funds are still in existence before you formulate your proposal. There will also continue to be new funding bodies set up in the future, be aware of these agencies by following industry newspapers. You often have a better chance of receiving funds from a newly created funding body as competition isn't as steep in the beginning.

I must tell you the road ahead will be complicated. There will be many times when you want to give up. Before you give up, re-evaluate your idea to understand why it isn't selling. Is it because there is no market for the idea? Or is it because your proposal does not state clearly enough what you are trying to achieve? Nine times out of ten it is because there aren't broadcasters looking for the type of material you're offering. Be wise, check the marketplace before formulating programming ideas. If you do it the other way around by coming up with an idea first then trying to sell it to broadcasters, this is often like trying to stick a round peg into a square hole. You will be trying to force an idea onto the marketplace that is not wanted by buyers. If this happens to you, learn from your mistakes and try again. Above all else, don't give up.

Finding broadcasters and financing for your program or series idea will be long and frustrating. Just remember, if you work hard, research your market, and be tenacious, you are bound to eventually succeed.

Re-evaluate Your Idea

Canadian National Television Broadcasters

Organization	Category	Mandate	Contact Information
Bravo!	National Cable Broadcaster	Specializing in arts and entertainment programming.	299 Queen St. W. Toronto, ON M5V 2Z5 t: 416-591-7400 f: 416-591-8497 www.bravo.ca
Bravo! Fact		Bravo Fact is a foundation to assist producers and Canadian arts associations to produce short programs on dance, music, spoken word and visual arts to be broadcast on Bravo.	Bravo! Fact t: 416-591-7400 f: 416-591-5117 www.bravo.ca/bravofact/
CBC Canadian Broadcasting Corporation	National Public Broadcaster	Network programming that covers all genres including news, sports, documentaries, entertainment and children's programming.	P.O. Box 500 Station A Toronto, ON M5W 1E6 t: 416-205-3311 www.cbc.ca/tv Contact individual departments for fax numbers.

Individual CBC Strands that Buy Programming from Independent Producers			
Organization	Category	Mandate	Contact Information
Man Alive	Documentary Series	Documentary series on stories of the spirit.	Documentary Unit CBC P.O. Box 500 Station A Toronto, ON M5W 1E6 t: 416-205-3056 f: 416-205-3199 www.tv.cbc.ca/manalive
Witness	Documentary Series	Documentary series featuring controversial, human and universal subjects.	Documentary Unit CBC P.O. Box 500 Station A Toronto, ON M5W 1E6 t: 416-205-8838 f: 416-205-8842 www.tv.cbc.ca/witness
CBC Newsworld	National Cable Broadcaster	24 hour news programming.	P.O. Box 500 Station A Toronto, ON M5W 1E6 t: 416-205-3311 f: 416-205-6080 www.newsworld.cbc.ca
Newsworld Strands that Buy Programming from Independent Producers			
Roughcuts	Documentary Series	Documentary series featuring original,	Documentary Unit P.O. Box 500

Organization	Category	Mandate	Contact Information
		edgy and experimental documentaries.	Station A Toronto, ON M5W 1E6 t: 416-205-6643 f: 416-205-8842 www.newsworld.cbc.ca/rougcuts
CanWest Global	National Private Broadcaster	Programming that covers all genres including news, sports, documentaries, entertainment and children's programming.	81 Barber Green Rd. Don Mills, ON M3C 2A2 t: 416-446-5311 f: 416-446-5502
The Comedy Network	National Cable Broadcaster	Channel dedicated to comedy programming.	P.O. Box 1000 Station O Toronto, ON M4A 2W3 t: 416-332-5300 f: 416-332-5301 www.the comedy network.ca
CTV Television Inc.	National Private Broadcaster	Programming that covers all genres including news, sports, documentaries, entertainment and children's programming.	P.O. Box 9 Station O Toronto, ON M5B 2N8 t: 416-299-2000 f: 416-299-2643 www.ctv.ca
The Discovery Channel	National Cable Broadcaster	Programming on themes of nature,	2225 Sheppard Ave.E. Ste. 100

Organization	Category	Mandate	Contact Information
		environment, science and technology, adventure, people and places.	North York, ON M2J 5C2 t: 416-494-2929 f: 416-490-7067 www.discovery.ca
The Family Channel	National Cable Broadcaster	Channel dedicated to children's and family programming.	BCE Place 181 Bay St. P.O. Box 787 Toronto, ON M5J 2T3 t: 416-956-2030 f: 416-956-2035 www.familychannel.ca
HGTV Home & Garden Television	National Cable Broadcaster	Programming evolves around five themes: gardening, building, home decorating, hobbies and crafts.	1155 Leslie St. Toronto, ON M3C 2J6 t: 416-444-9494 f: 416-444-0018 www.hgtv.com
History Television	National Cable Broadcaster	Channel devoted to historical programming.	121 Bloor St. E. Ste. 200 Toronto, ON M4W 3M5 t: 416-967-0022 f: 416-967-0044 www.historytelevision.ca
The Life Network	National Cable Broadcaster	Information and lifestyle programming.	1155 Leslie St. Toronto, ON M3C 2J6 t: 416-444-9494 f: 416-444-0018 www.lifenetwork.ca

Organization	Category	Mandate	Contact Information
OLN Outdoor Life Network	National Cable Broadcaster	Programming about the great outdoors and adventure activities.	P.O. Box 9 Station O Toronto, ON M4A 2M9 t: 416-332-5616 f: 416-332-5624 www.ctv.ca
Prime TV	National Cable Broadcaster	Programming catering to more mature audiences with emphasis on family viewing.	81 Barber Greene Rd. Don Mills, ON M3C 2A2 t: 416-446-5311 f: 416-443-6070
RDI Le Reseau de l'information	National Cable Broadcaster	24 Hour news programming broadcast in the French language.	Société Radio-Canada 1400 René-Lévesque Blvd. E Montreal, QC H2L 2M2 t: 514-597-7734 f: 514-597-3920 www.radio-canada.ca
Showcase Television	National Cable Broadcaster	Programming centred on Canadian series and foreign films.	121 Bloor St. E. Ste. 200 Toronto, ON M4W 3M5 t: 416-967-0022 f: 416-967-0044 www.showcase.ca
Space: The Imagination Station	National Cable Broadcaster	Programming devoted to space related topics.	299 Queen St. W. Toronto, ON M5V 2Z5

Organization	Category	Mandate	Contact Information
			t: 416-591-7400 f: 416-591-6619 www.spacecast.com
Teletoon	National Cable Broadcaster	Programming dedicated to the animated form.	BCE Place 181 Bay St. Toronto, ON M5J 2T3 t: 416-956-2060 f: 416-956-2070 www.teletoon.com
Treehouse TV	National Cable Broadcaster	Broadcasting programs suitable for preschool children.	64 Jefferson Ave, Unit 18 Toronto, ON M6K 3H3 t: 416-534-1191 f: 416-533-0346 www.treehousetv.com
TSN The Sports Network	National Cable Broadcaster	24 hour sports programming.	2225 Sheppard Ave.E. Ste. 100 Willowdale, ON M2J 5C2 t: 416-494-1212 f: 416-490-7040 www.tsn.ca
Vision TV	National Cable Broadcaster	Programming related to faith and social issues as well as documentaries, music, drama, films.	80 Bond St. Toronto, ON M5B 1X2 t: 416-368-3194 f: 416-368-9774 www.visiontv.ca

Organization	Category	Mandate	Contact Information
WTN Women's Television Network	National Cable Broadcaster	Programming and entertainment of particular interest to women.	1661 Portage Ave. Ste. 300 Winnipeg, MB R3J 3P7 t: 204-783-5116 f: 204-774-3227 www.wtn.ca
YTV	National Cable Broadcaster	Specializing in dramatic and comedic, series targeted to youths 9 to 14.	64 Jefferson Ave. Unit 18 Toronto, ON M6K 3H3 t: 416-534-1191 f: 416-533-0346 www.ytv.com

Canadian Provincial Television Broadcasters and Provincial Funding Agencies

Organization	Category	Mandate	Contact Information
British Columbia			
British Columbia Cultural Services administers programs of: BC Arts Council Project Assistance for Media Artists	Government	Development and production financing for innovative, experimental and non-industrial works by British Columbia residents. www.sbtc.gov.bc.ca/culture/csb/bcac.htm	c/o Media Arts Box 9819 Stn. Prov. Govt Victoria, BC V8W 9W3 t: 250-356-1718 f: 250-387-4099
British Columbia Film Production Financing Program Film Incentive B.C.	Government (tax credit)	Development and production financing for projects produced by British Columbia residents. Production financing for film and television projects.	2225 W. Broadway Vancouver, BC V6K 2E4 t: 604-736-7997 f: 604-736-7290 www.bcfilm.bc.ca
BC Heritage	Government	Provides funding for projects on B.C.	c/o Heritage Branch P.O. Box 9818

Organization	Category	Mandate	Contact Information
		historical or cultural subjects.	Stn. Prov. Govt Victoria, BC V8W 9W3 t: 800-663-7867 or 250-356-1433 f: 250-356-7796 www.heritage.gov.bc.ca
BC TEL New Media and Broadcast Fund	Private Fund	Financing for new media productions which have a broadcast component.	5-3777 Kingsway Burnaby, BC V5H 3Z7 t: 604-432-2041 f: 604-439-7354 www.bctel.com/b_creative
BCTV (member of WIC Entertainment)	Regional Broadcaster	Broadcasts a mixture of network and regionally produced programming.	P.O. Box 4700 Vancouver, BC V6B 4A3 t: 604-420-2288 f: 604-421-9427 www.TVFORBC. com
CHEK TV (member of WIC Entertainment)	Regional Broadcaster	Broadcasts a mixture of network and regionally produced programming.	780 Kings Rd. Victoria, BC V8T 5A2 t: 888-389-6460 or 250-383-2435 f: 250-384-7766 www.chektv.com
CIVT-TV (CTV affiliate station)	Regional Broadcaster	Broadcasts a mixture of network and regionally produced programming.	750 Burrard St Ste. 300 Vancouver, BC V6Z 1X5

Organization	Category	Mandate	Contact Information
			t: 604-608-2868 f: 604-608-2698 www.vancouvertelevision.com
Knowledge Network	Provincial Educational Broadcaster	Mandate is to offer programs of an educational nature to the residents of British Columbia.	4355 Mathissi Pl. Burnaby, BC V5G 4S8 t: 604-431-3226 f: 604-431-3387 www.knowtv.com
Prairies			
A Channel Drama Fund	Regional Broadcaster	Development and production funding for Alberta-based productions including movies, mini-series, music and variety programs for broad-cast on the A-Channel.	A-Channel Calgary/CKAL 535-7th Ave. S.W. Calgary, AB T2P 0Y4 t: 403-508-2222 f: 403-508-2224 www.a-channel.com A-Channel Edmonton/CKEM 10212 Jasper Ave. Edmonton, AB T5J 5A3 t: 780-424-2222 f: 780-424-0357 www.a-channel.com
Access -The Education	Provincial Educational	Broadcasts a variety of educational programs	3720-76th Ave. Edmonton, AB

Organization	Category	Mandate	Contact Information
Station	Broadcaster	including, dramas documentaries, and entertainment.	T6B 2N9 t: 780-440-7777 f: 780-440-8899 www.accesstv.ab.ca
AFDP Alberta Film Development Program	Government	Grants for film and television projects produced by Alberta-based producers.	c/o Alberta Community Development Arts & Libraries 901 Standard Life Centre 10405 Jasper Ave. Edmonton, AB T5J 4R7 t: 780-427-6315 f: 780-422-9132
Alberta Foundation for the Arts	Government	Funds available for films and video containing artistic merit by Alberta-based producers.	901 Standard Life Centre 10405 Jasper Ave. Edmonton, AB T5J 4R7 t: 780-427-9968 f: 780-422-1162 www.affta.ab.ca
CFCN-TV (CTV affiliate station)	Regional Broadcaster	Broadcasting a mixture of network and regionally produced programming.	80 Patina Rise S.W. Calgary, AB T3H 2W4 t: 403-240-5600 f: 403-240-5711 www.ctv.ca
CFCN Production Fund	Private Fund	Funds available for programming for later broadcast on CFCN.	

Organization	Category	Mandate	Contact Information
CFRN-TV (CTV affiliate station) CFRN Production Fund	Regional Broadcaster	Broadcasting a mixture of network and regionally produced programming. Funds available for programming for later broadcast on CFRN.	18520 Stoney Plain Edmonton, AB T5S 1A8 t: 780-483-3311 f: 780-484-4426 www.ctv.ca
CHAT-TV (CBC affiliate station)	Regional Broadcaster	Broadcasting a mixture of network and regionally produced programming.	1111 Kingsway Box 1270 Medicine Hat, AB T1A 7H5 t: 403-529-1270 f: 403-529-1292 www.cbc.ca/tv
CKY (CTV affiliate station)	Regional Broadcaster	Broadcasting a mixture of network and regionally produced programming.	Polopark Winnipeg, MB R3G 0L7 t: 204-788-3300 f: 204-788-3399
CICT (member of WIC Entertainment)	Regional Broadcaster	Broadcasting a mixture of network and regionally produced programming.	222-23rd St., N.E. Calgary, AB T2E 7N2 t: 403-235-7777 f: 403-248-0252
CISA WIC Entertainment	Regional Broadcaster	Broadcasting a mixture of network and regionally	1401-28th St. N. Lethbridge, AB T1H 6H9

Organization	Category	Mandate	Contact Information
		produced programming.	t: 403-327-1521 f: 403-320-2620 www.cisatv.com
CKRD (CBC affiliate station)	Regional Broadcaster	Broadcasting a mixture of network and regionally produced programming.	2840 Brenner Ave. Box 5555 Red Deer, AB T4N 5H6 t: 403-346-2573 f: 403-346-9980 www.cbc.ca/tv
CKSA (CBC affiliate station)	Regional Broadcaster	Broadcasting a mixture of network and regionally produced programming.	Radio/TV Building 5026-50th St. Lloydminster, AB T9V 1P3 t: 780-875-3321 f: 780-875-4704 www.cbc.ca/tv
CTV Saskatchewan Program Development Fund	Regional Broadcaster	Provides funding for productions to be aired on CTV by Saskatchewan-based writers and producers.	216 1st Ave. N. Saskatoon, SK S7K 3W3 t: 306-665-8600 f: 306-665-0450 www.ctv.ca
ITV-Edmonton	Regional Broadcaster	Broadcasting a mixture of network and regionally produced programming.	5325 Allard Way Edmonton, AB T6H 5B8 t: 780-436-1250 f: 780-438-8448 www.itv.ca

Organization	Category	Mandate	Contact Information
Manitoba Arts Council	Government	Development and production funding for innovative film and video projects.	525-93 Lombard Winnipeg, MB R3B 3B1 t: 204-945-2237 f: 204-945-5925 www.artscouncil.mb.ca
The Film/ Video Script Development Grant		Financing for the development of scripts.	
The Film/ Video Production Grant		Production grants for documentaries, drama, animation and innovative projects.	
CIDO Manitoba Cultural Industries Development Office	Government	Funding for film and video projects by Manitoba-based producers.	c/o Business Development Bank of Canada Bow Valley Square 1 202-6th Ave. S.W. Ste. 1500, 15th flr. Calgary, AB T2P 2R9 t: 888-INFO-BDC or 403-292-5000 f: 403-292-6616 www.bdc.ca http://cbsc.org/alberta/bis/1086.html
Manitoba Film and Sound Corp.	Government	Provides development and production funds for film and	333-93 Lombard Winnipeg, MB R3B 3B1

Organization	Category	Mandate	Contact Information
		television productions by Manitoba-based producers.	t: 204-947-2040 f: 204-956-5261 www.mbfilmsound.mb.ca
Development Financing Program Production Financing Program Manitoba Film & Video Production Tax Credit		Development financing for film and television projects. Production financing for film and television projects.	
MTN Manitoba Television Network (Craig Broadcasting)	Regional Broadcaster	Broadcasts a mixture of network and regionally produced programming.	*Portage La Prairie:* 350 River Rd. Box 13000 Portage LaPrairie, MB R1N 3V3 t: 204-239-1113 f: 204-857-9295 *Winnipeg:* Ste.100 167 Lombard Ave. Winnipeg, MB R3B 0T6 t: 204-947-9613 f: 204-956-0811

Organization	Category	Mandate	Contact Information
RDTV (Member of WIC Entertainment)	Regional Broadcaster	Broadcasts a mixture of network and regionally produced programming.	2840 Bremner Ave. Red Deer, AB T4R 1M9 t: 403-346-2573 f: 403-346-9980
Saskatchewan Arts Board Media Arts Grant	Government	Funding for artistic film and television productions by Saskatchewan-based producers.	T.C. Douglas Bldg. 3475 Albert St. 3rd Flr Regina, SK S4S 6X6 t: 800-667-7526 or 306-787-4056 f: 306-787-4199
SCN Saskatchewan Communications Network	Provincial Educational Broadcaster	Broadcasting a mixture of educational and entertainment programming.	North Block 2440 Broad St. Regina, SK S4P 3V7 t: 800-667-5055 or 306-787-0490 f: 306-787-0265 www.scn.sk.ca
SaskCulture (Cultural Assistance Program)	Government	Supports culturally relevant projects that stress public participation and access to cultural activity.	210-438 Victoria E. Regina, SK S4N 0N7 t: 306-780-9284 f: 306-780-9252 www.saskculture.sk.ca
Saskatchewan Cultural Industries	Government	Contributes funds for the marketing and promotion of film or	c/o Saskatchewan Economic & Co-operative

Organization	Category	Mandate	Contact Information
		video projects by Saskatchewan-based producers.	Development 1919 Saskatchewan Regina, SK S4P 3V7 t: 306-787-4707 f: 306-787-1620 www.gov.sk.ca
SaskFILM Saskatchewan Film & Video Development Corp. Scriptwriters Fund Saskatchewan Film Employment Tax Credit	Government	Development, production and marketing loans for Saskatchewan-based producers of film and video.	2445-13th Ave. Ste. 340 Regina, SK S4P 0W1 t: 306-347-3456 f: 306-359-7768
Saskatchewan Program Development Fund (CFQC-TV, CTV affiliate)	Private Fund	Funding towards the development of programs and scripts by Saskatchewan-based producers for later broadcast by CFQC.	216 1st Ave. N. Saskatoon, SK S7K 3W3 t: 306-665-9233 f: 306-665-0450
Superchannel (subsidiary of WIC)	Pay Movie Channel in Western Canada	Funding for the development and production of	c/o WIC Premium Television 5324 Calgary Trail

Organization	Category	Mandate	Contact Information
		dramatic series, movies and children's programming for later broadcast on the Superchannel.	Ste. 200 Edmonton, AB T6H 4J8 t: 780-430-2800 f: 780-437-3188 www.premiumtv.com
WIC (Western International Communications Ltd.)	Private Fund	Funding for feature films, television series, MOW's, mini-series and seasonal dramas.	Entertainment 5325 Allard Way Edmonton, AB T6H 5B8 t: 780-438-8555 f: 780-438-8495 www.wic.ca
Ontario			
CFPL (CHUM-CITY affiliate station)	Regional Broadcaster	Broadcasts a mixture of network and regionally produced programming.	1 Communications Rd. Box 5810 London, ON N6A 6E9 t: 519-686-8822 f: 519-686-0597
CHEX (CBC affiliate station)	Regional Broadcaster	Broadcasts a mixture of network and regionally produced programming.	Box 4150 1925 Television Rd. Peterborough, ON K9J 6Z9 t: 705-742-0451 f: 705-742-7274
CICI/CKNC (CTV affiliate station)	Regional Broadcaster	Broadcasts a mixture of network and regionally produced	699 Frood Rd. Sudbury, ON P3C 5A3

Organization	Category	Mandate	Contact Information
		programming.	t: 705-674-8301 f: 705-671-2444
CITY TV	Regional Broadcaster	Broadcasting a large genre of programming including news, sports, films and entertainment based programs.	299 Queen St. W. Toronto, ON M5V 2Z5 t: 416-591-5757 f: 416-591-8497 www.citytv.com
CJOH (CTV affiliate station) CJOH Development Fund	Regional Broadcaster	Funding for projects produced by Eastern Ontario- and Western Quebec-based producers.	Box 5813 Merivale Depot Nepean, ON K2C 3G6 t: 613-224-1313 f: 613-274-4280
CKCO (CTV affiliate station)	Regional Broadcaster	Broadcasts a mixture of network and regionally produced programming.	864 King St. W. P.O. Box 91206 Stn. C Kitchener, ON N2G 4E9 t: 519-578-1313 f: 519-743-8857 www.ctv.ca
CKPR/CHFD (CBC affiliate stations)	Regional Broadcaster	Broadcasts a mixture of network and regionally produced programming.	c/o Thunder Bay Television 87 North Hill St. Thunder Bay, ON P7A 5V6 t: 807-346-2600 f: 807-345-9923 www.cbc.ca/tv

Organization	Category	Mandate	Contact Information
CKVR (CHUM-CITY affiliate station)	Regional Broadcaster	Broadcasting a mixture of network and regionally produced programs.	P.O. Box 519 Barrie, ON L4M 4T9 t: 705-734-3300 f: 705-733-0302 www.thenewvr.ca
OFDC Ontario Film Development Corp. Ontario Film & Television Tax Credit Program	Government	Administration of the labour tax credit for Ontario-based productions.	175 Bloor St. E. North Tower Ste. 300 Toronto, ON M4W 3R8 t: 416-314-6858 f: 416-314-6876 www.to-ontfilm.com
Ontario Arts Council Artists' Film and Video Grants First Projects Film & Video	Government	Grants to Ontario-based artists using film and video as a means of creative expression.	151 Bloor St. W. 6th Flr. Toronto, ON M5S 1T6 t: 800-387-0058 or 416-961-1660 f: 416-961-7796 www.arts.on.ca
ONTV (member of WIC entertainment)	Regional Broadcaster	Broadcasting a mixture of network and regionally produced programming.	163 Jackson St. W. Box 2230, Stn A Hamilton, ON L8N 3A6 t: 905-522-1101 f: 905-523-8011 www.ontv.ca

Organization	Category	Mandate	Contact Information
TFO (TVO French-language network)	Provincial Educational Broadcaster	Broadcasting educational and entertainment programming in the French language.	2180 Yonge St. Toronto, ON M4S 2B9 t: 416-484-2600 f: 416-484-6285 www.tfo.org
Toronto Arts Council	Government	Funding for projects demonstrating artistic merit by Toronto-based producers.	141 Bathurst St. Ste. 101 Toronto, ON M5V 2R2 t: 416-392-6802 f: 416-392-6920 www.torontoartscouncil.org
TVOntario	Provincial Educational Broadcaster	Broadcasting educational and entertainment programming.	2180 Yonge St. Toronto, ON M4S 2B9 t: 800-INFO-TVO 416-484-2600 f: 416-484-6285 www.tvontario.org
Quebec			
A & E/ Canal D Canadian Production Fund	Private Fund	Funds for Canadian programming to air on both A&E and Canal D.	A & E TV 235 E. 45th St. New York, NY USA 10017 t: 212-210-9001 f: 212-210-9077 www.a&e.com
Canal Vie	Provincial Cable	Mandate is to broadcast lifestyle	1717 René Levesque est

Organization	Category	Mandate	Contact Information
	Broadcaster	programming.	Bur. 50￼ Montreal, QC￼ H2L 4T9￼ t: 514-529-3233￼ f: 514-529-3236￼ www.servicevie.com
CFCF￼ (CTV affiliate station)	Regional Broadcaster	Broadcasting a mixture of network and regionally produced programming.	405 Ogilvy Ave.￼ Montréal, QC￼ H3N 1M4￼ t: 514-273-6311￼ f: 514-276-1212
FIDEC￼ Financière des entreprises culturelles	Private and Public Fund	Mixture of private and public funds invested in film and television productions in the form of gap financing, rights acquisition and production funding.	215 St.-Jacques St.￼ Bur. 800￼ Montréal, QC￼ H2Y 1M6￼ t: 514-940-7501￼ f: 514-940-1528￼ www.fidecinvest.com
Musimax	Provincial Cable Channel	Mandate is to broadcast music related programming in the form of videos and entertainment programming.	355 St. Catherine ouest￼ Montréal, QC￼ H3B 1A5￼ t: 514-284-7587￼ f: 514-284-1889￼ www.musicplus.com
Quebec Refundable Production Tax Credit	Government	Labour tax credit for Quebec-based productions.	c/o Société de développement des entreprises culturelles

Organization	Category	Mandate	Contact Information
			215 St.-Jacques St. Bur. 800 Montréal, QC H2Y 1M6 t: 514-841-2200 f: 514-841-8606
Canal D	Provincial Cable Channel	Broadcasts documentary and entertainment programs on a variety of topics.	2100 rue Ste. Catherine, ouest Bur. 800 Montréal, QC H3H 2T3 t: 514-939-3150 f: 514-939-3151
Canal Famille	Provincial Cable Channel	Broadcasts family entertainment.	2100 rue Ste- Catherine, ouest Bur. 800 Montréal, QC H3H 2T3 t: 514-939-3150 f: 514-939-3151
RDS Le reseau des sports	Provincial Cable Channel	Broadcasts sports programming in the French language.	1755 René Levesque est Ste. 300 Montréal, QC H2K 4P6 t: 514-599-2244 f: 514-599-2299 www.rds.ca
SODEC Société	Government	Development, production and	215 St.-Jacques St. Bur. 800

Organization	Category	Mandate	Contact Information
Developpe-ment des Entreprises Culturelles Quebec Refundable Tax Credit Program		marketing funds for Quebec-based producers.	Montréal, QC H2Y 1M6 t: 514-841-2200 f: 514-841-8606
Societe Radio-Canada	Provincial Government Broadcaster	Broadcasting a wide genre of programming from news, sports, children's programming, documentaries and entertainment in the French language.	1400 René Levesque est Case postale 6000 Montréal, QC H3C 3A8 t: 514-597-6000 f: 514-597-5551 www.radiocanada.com
Television Quatre Saisons	Provincial Broadcaster	Mandate is to offer alternative programming to francophone viewers across Quebec.	405 ave. Ogilvy Montréal, QC H3N 2Y4 t: 514-271-3535 f: 514-495-7330
Tele-Quebec	Provincial Educational Broadcaster	Broadcasts programming on information, youth, culture, education and fiction.	1000 rue Fullum Montréal, QC H2K 3L7 t: 514-521-2424 f: 514-873-7739 or 514-525-5511
TV5	Provincial Cable Channel	News and information programming	1755 Rene Levesque est

Organization	Category	Mandate	Contact Information
		presented in the French language.	Ste. 101 Montréal, QC H2K 4P6 t: 514-522-5322 f: 514-522-6572 www.tv5.org
TVA	Provincial Broadcaster	News, information and entertainment programming presented in the French language.	1600 boul. De Maisonneuve Est Montréal, QC H2L 4P2 t: 514-526-9251 f: 514-598-6078 www.tva.ca
East Coast			
Canada/ Newfoundland Cooperation Agreement on Cultural Development	Government	Marketing and promotional funds for film and video for Newfoundland-based producers.	P.O.Box 1854 Arts and Culture Centre 3rd floor St. John's, NF A1C 5P9 t: 709-772-2285 f: 709-772-2026
Canada/ Nova Scotia Agreement on Cultural Development	Government	Funds to assist in the promotion and marketing of films and videos from Nova Scotia-based producers.	P.O. Box 39 Halifax, NS B3J 2L4 t: 902-424-2118 f: 902-424-0645
CBC Newfoundland	Provincial Public	Broadcasting a mixture of network and	95 University Ave. P.O. Box 12010

Organization	Category	Mandate	Contact Information
	Broadcaster	regionally produced programming.	Stn. A St. John's, NF A1B 3T8 t: 709-576-5000 f: 709-576-5144
CBC Maritimes	Provincial Public Broadcaster	Broadcasting a mixture of network and regionally produced programming.	1840 Bell Rd. Halifax, NS B3J 3E9 t: 902-420-8311 f: 902-420-4010
CJCH (ATV/ASN) (CTV affiliate station)	Regional Broadcaster	Broadcasting a mixture of network and regionally produced programming.	2885 Robie St. Halifax, NS B3K 5Z4 t: 902-453-4000 f: 902-454-3302
Enterprise P.E.I.	Government	Provides funds for television and film productions produced or co-produced by a PEI production company.	P.O. Box 910 Charlottetown, PEI C1A 7L9 t: 902-368-6300 f: 902-368-6301 www.gov.pe.ca
Film New Brunswick- New Brunswick's Labour Incentive Film Tax Credit	Government	Tax Credit as well as funding for projects by New Brunswick-based producers.	P.O. Box 5001 Moncton, NB E1C 8R3 t: 506-869-6868 f: 506-869-6840 www.gov.nb.ca\filmnb

Organization	Category	Mandate	Contact Information
Fundy Community Television	Regional Broadcaster	Broadcasts regional programming.	377 York St. Fredericton, NB E3B 5B1 t: 506-462-3637 f: 506-452-2846 www.Fundy.ca
Fundy Communications Program Development Fund		Provides funds for educational, informational and new media projects in the Atlantic provinces.	c/o CIFVF 666 Kirkwood Ave. Suite 203 Ottawa, ON K1Z 5X9 t: 613-729-1900 f: 613-729-4610 www.cifvf.ca
Newfoundland & Labrador Arts Council	Government	Funding for projects of artistic merit by Newfoundland-based producers.	PO Box 98 Station C St. John's, NF A1C 5H5 t: 709-726-2212 f: 709-726-0619 www.nlac.nf.ca
Newfoundland and Labrador Film Development Corp. Film Tax Credit	Government	Funding for film and television productions by Newfoundland-based producers as well as the administration of the labour-based tax credit.	197/99 Water St. St. John's, NF A1C 1B4 t: 709-738-FILM f: 709-739-1680

Organization	Category	Mandate	Contact Information
Nova Scotia Arts Council	Government	Funding for artistic projects by Nova Scotia-based producers.	1660 Hollis St. Ste. 302 P.O. Box 1559 CRNO Halifax, NS B3J 2Y3 t: 902-422-1123 f: 902-422-1445
Nova Scotia Film Development Corp. Nova Scotia Film Industry Tax Credit	Government	Development and production funds for projects by Nova Scotia-based producers as well as the administration of the tax credit program.	1724 Granville St. Halifax NS B3J 1X5 t: 902-424-7177 f: 902-424-0617 www.film.ns.ca
Northwest Territories			
NT: Assistance for Artistic Projects	Government	Providing funding for film and video projects by residents of the Northwest Territories.	Cultural Affairs Culture & Heritage Education Culture & Employment Government of the N.W. Territories P.O. Box 1320 Yellowknife, NT X1A 2L9 t: 867-920-3103 f: 867-873-0205

Organization	Category	Mandate	Contact Information
TVNC Television Northern Canada (NAME CHANGE IN 1999 - TO) APTN Aboriginal Peoples Television Network	Regional Broadcaster	Aboriginal, English and French programming including children's, educational, documentary and variety.	Communication Centre 5120-49th St. Box #93 Yellowknife, NT X1A 1P8 t: 867-873-9691 f: 867-873-3786 www.tvnc.ca

National Funding Bodies
(Comprises Government Funding Agencies & Television Industry Funds)

Organization	Category	Mandate	Contact Information
Astral Programming Fund	Private Fund	Funds available for English and French language documentaries.	c/o Canal D 2100 rue Sainte-Catherine ouest Bur. 800 Montreal, QC t: 514-939-3150 f: 514-939-3151 www.astral.com
Bell Broadcast and New Media Fund	Private Fund	Provides grants for television productions that possess a new media component and are licensed by a broadcaster.	c/o The Independent Production Fund 2 Carlton St. Ste. 1709 Toronto, ON M5B 1J3 t: 416-977-8154 f: 416-977-0694 *In Montréal:* 1255 boul. Laird Bur 275 Ville Mont-Royal,QC H3P 2T1 t: 514-737-1337 f: 514-737-9008 www.bell.ca/fund
Canada Council for the Arts	Government	To encourage artistic creation, research and experimentation	c/o Media Arts Section 350 Albert St.

Organization	Category	Mandate	Contact Information
		through the production of video, film, and media arts.	Box 1047 Ottawa, ON K1P 5V8 t: 800-263-5588 or 613-566-4414 f: 613-566-4409 www.canadacouncil.ca
Grants to Film /Video Artists		Grants for development and production to assist artists working in film and video.	
Grants for First Productions in Media Arts		Grants to assist artists making their first video or media arts production.	
Aboriginal Media Arts Program		Grants for aboriginal artists in film, video and new media.	
CAVCO Canadian Film or Video Production Tax Credit Program

Federal Tax Credit | Federal Government Program | Federal tax credit program for the refund of Canadian labour expenses for film and video productions. | c/o CAVCO Les Terrasses de la Chaudière 15 Eddy St. 6th Flr. Hull, QC K1A 0M5 t: 819-997-6861 1-888-433-2200 f: 819-997-6892 www.pch.gc.ca cavco |

Organization	Category	Mandate	Contact Information
Canadian Heritage Multi-culturalism Program	Government	Funding body which provides grants to film and video makers for culturally relevant projects. *Western:* *Prairies & Northwest Territories:* *Ontario:* *Quebec:*	www.pch.gc.ca *Regional Offices:* Rm. 300- 300 West Georgia St Vancouver, BC V6B 6C6 t: 604-666-0176 f: 604-666-3508 275 Portage Ave. 2nd Flr. Winnipeg, MB R3C 3R5 t: 204-983-3601 f: 204-984-6996 4900 Yonge St. Ph level Toronto, ON M2N 6A4 t: 416-954-2738 f: 416-954-4515 200 René-Levésque Blvd.W. West Tower, 6th Flr. Montréal, QC H2Z 1X4 t: 514-283-2332 f: 514-283-3036

Organization	Category	Mandate	Contact Information
		Atlantic:	1045 Main St. Moncton, NB E1C 1H1 t: 506-851-7066 f: 506-851-7079
Canadian Studies and Youth Programmes (Part of Canadian Heritage)	Government	Provides funding for cultural projects on Canadian Heritage.	Canadian Studies Program Department of Canadian Heritage 15 Eddy St. 7th Flr Hull, QC K1A 0M4 t: 819-994-1544 f: 819-994-1314
CanWest Global Development Fund	Private Fund	Development loans for projects to be licensed by CanWest Global in the areas of drama, comedy, children's programming and documentaries.	81 Barber Green Rd. Don Mills, ON M3C 2A2 t: 416-446-5526 f: 416-446-5398
CIDA Canadian International Development Agency	Government	Funds to aid in the development and production of film, video and multi-media with a special emphasis on the role Canadians make in developing countries.	c/o Communications Branch 200 Promenade de Portage Hull, QC K1A 0G4 t: 819-997-1663 f: 819-953-4933 http://w3. acdi-cida.gc.da/dip

Organization	Category	Mandate	Contact Information
CIFVF Canadian Independent Film & Video Fund	Private Fund	To foster the development and production of films and videos designed for the non-theatrical markets.	666 Kirkwood Ave. Ste. 203 Ottawa, ON K1Z 5X9 t: 613-729-1900 f: 613-729-4610 www.cifvf.ca
Cogeco Program Development Fund	Private Fund	Funding for the development of dramatic series, movies of the week, and miniseries.	c/o The Independent Production Fund 2 Carlton St. Ste. 1709 Toronto, ON M5B 1J3 t: 416- 977-8966 f: 416-977-0694
Cogeco Production Program	Private Fund	Equity financing for the production of movies of the week, mini-series and pilots for dramatic series.	*In Montréal:* c/o The Independent Production Fund 1255 boul. Laird Bur 275 Ville Mont-Royal, QC H3P 2T1 t: 514-737-9969 f: 514-737-9008 www.ipf.ca
CTF Canadian Television Fund	Consortium of Government and Private Funds	Provides funding in the categories of drama, children's, documentary, variety and performing arts.	45 Charles St. E. Ste. 802 Toronto, ON M4Y 1S2 t: 877-975-0766 or

Organization	Category	Mandate	Contact Information
License Fee Program Equity Investment Program (Administered by Telefilm Canada)			416-975-0766 f: 416-975-2680 www.canadiantelevisionfund.ca
IPF Independent Production Fund	Private Fund	Mandate is to assist in the funding of Canadian dramatic television series for private broadcasters. *In Montreal:*	2 Carlton St. Ste. 1709 Toronto, ON M5B 1J3 t: 416- 977-8966 f: 416-977-0694 www.ipf.ca 1255 boul. Laird Bur 275 Ville Mont-Royal, QC H3P 2T1 t: 514-737-9969 f: 514-737-9008
NFB National Film Board	Government	Funding for culturally relevant documentaries, children's programming, animation and multi-media projects.	*Operational Headquarters* Norman-McLaren Building 3155 Côte de Liess St-Laurent, QC H4N 2N4

Organization	Category	Mandate	Contact Information
			t: 800-267-7710 or 514-283-9000 f: 514-283-5556
ACIC - French Program's Aide au Cinema Independent Canada		Funding for French-language documentaries or short dramas by new producers.	*Pacific Centre:* #200-1385 West 8th Ave. Vancouver, BC V6H 3V9 t: 604-666-3838 f: 604-666-1569
Aboriginal Filmmaker's Program		Funding for projects by Aboriginal filmmakers.	*North West Centre:* 10815-104th Ave. Rm. 100 Edmonton, AB T5J 4N6 t: 780-495-3013 f: 780-495-6412
FAP - English Programs Filmmaker Assistance Program		Funding for English-language documentaries.	*Prairie Centre:* 245 Main St. Winnipeg, MB R3C 1A7 t: 204-983-7996 f: 204-983-0742
		Ontario Centre:	150 John St. Toronto, ON M5V 3C3 t: 416-973-3012 f: 416-973-9640
		Atlantic Centre:	Queen's Court 5475 Spring Garden

Organization	Category	Mandate	Contact Information
			2nd Flr. Halifax, N.S B3J 1G2 t: 902-426-6000 f: 902-426-8901 www.nfb.ca
Rogers Documentary Fund Rogers Telefund	Private Fund	Provides grants for documentaries licensed by broadcasters.	333 Bloor St. E. 9th Flr. Toronto, ON M4W 1G9 t: 416-935-2555 f: 416-935-2527 www.rogers.com
Shaw Children's Programming Initiative Shaw Television Broadcast Fund Dr. Geoffrey R. Conway Programming Fund	Private Fund	Mandate is to assist in the financing of children's, youth and family programming. Mandate is to assist in the financing of children's, youth and family programming. Financing for pre-school and primary school-age children's programming.	630-3rd Ave. SW Ste. 530 Calgary, AB T2P 4L4 t: 403-468-7115 f: 403-750-7482
Telefilm Canada	Government	To support the production of	*Head Office:* Tour de la Banque

Organization	Category	Mandate	Contact Information
		culturally relevant productions in the category of documentary, drama and children's programming.	Nationale 600 de la Gauchetière St.W. 14th Flr. Montréal, QC H3B 4L8 t: 800-567-0890 or 514-283-6363 f: 514-283-8212
Canadian Broadcast Program Development Fund		Development financing for television productions.	*West Coast Office:* 310-440 Cambie St. Vancouver, BC V6B 2N5 t: 800-663-7771 or 604-666-1566 f: 604-666-7754
Canadian Broadcast Production Fund		Equity financing for television productions.	*Ontario Office:* 2 Bloor St. W. 22nd Flr. Toronto, ON M4W 3E2 t: 800-463-4607 or 416-973-6436 f: 416-973-8606
		East Coast Office:	1684 Barrington St. 3rd Flr Halifax, NS B3J 2A2 t: 800-565-1773 or 902-426-8425 f: 902-426-4445 www.telefilm.gc.ca

Organization	Category	Mandate	Contact Information
VideoFact	Private Fund	Assistance for the production of music videos.	c/o Much Music 260 Richmond St. W. Ste. 501 Toronto, ON M5V 1W5 t: 416-596-8696 f: 416-596-6861 www.muchmusic.com
WIC Entertainment (Western International Communications Ltd.)	Private Fund	Development funding for feature films, television, series, MOW's mini-series and seasonal dramas to be broadcast on WIC.	1960- 505 Burrard St. Vancouver, BC V7X 1M6 t: 604-687-2844 f: 604-687-4118 www.wic.ca

Interim Financing

Organization	Category	Mandate	Contact Information
Banque Nationale de Paris	Bank Financing	Provides interim financing for animation and television series.	1981 McGill College Ave. BNP Tower Montreal, QC H3A 2W8 t: 514-285-6000 f: 514-285-6009
Bank of Nova Scotia	Bank Financing	Funding for film, television and multimedia projects.	Corporate Banking Media & Communications 44 King St. W. 16th Flr Toronto, ON M5H 1H1 t: 416-866-3332 f: 416-866-2010
Independent Film Financing	Private Funding (Through an agreement with an American bank.)	Offers interim financing and other financing options for television and film productions.	372 Richmond St .W. Ste. 306 Toronto, ON M5V 1X6 t: 416-598-3270 f: 416-598-5045
Malcolm Silver & Co.	Private Fund	Provides financing for film and television projects from producers with several projects in production.	194 Merton St. Ste. 210 Toronto, ON M4S 1A1 t: 416-488-3393 f: 416-488-5217 www.msilver.com

Organization	Category	Mandate	Contact Information
National Bank of Canada	Bank Financing	Provides interim financing for animation, television series and movies of the week. *Montréal Office:*	*Toronto Office:* 150 York St. Toronto, ON M5H 3S5 t: 416-864-7762 f: 416-864-7682 600 Rue de Chaussée de la Gauchetière ouest Montréal, QC H3B 4L2 t: 514-394-8474 f: 514-394-4144
Republic National Bank of New York (Canada)	Bank Financing	Funding for film and television projects.	150 Bloor St. W. Ste. M100 Toronto, ON M5S 2Y5 t: 416-968-7622 f: 416-968-7669
Royal Bank	Bank Financing	Funding for film, television and multi-media projects. *Montréal Office:*	*Toronto Office:* 5th Flr. South Tower 200 Bay St Toronto, ON M5J 2J5 t: 416-955-FILM f: 416-974-FILM www.RoyalBank.com 360 St. Jacques St. Montréal, QC H2Y 1P6 t: 514-874-CINE f: 514-874-5198

Organization	Category	Mandate	Contact Information
		Halifax Office:	Royal Bank Business Banking Centre Mezzanine Level 5161 George St. Halifax, NS B3J 1M7 t: 902-463-FILM f: 902-421-8139
		Regina Office:	2010 - 11th Ave. 8th Flr. P.O. Box 4422 Regina, SK S4P 3W7 t: 306-775-FILM f: 306-780-2523
		Vancouver Office:	Royal Bank Business Banking Centre 1025 W. Georgia St 2nd Flr. Vancouver, BC V6E 3N9 t: 604-684-FILM f: 604-665-6368
Toronto-Dominion Bank	Bank Financing	Interim financing for television and film productions.	*Toronto Office:* 141 Adelaide St. W. Toronto, ON M5H 3L5 t: 416-9TD-FILM f: 416-982-4330
		Montréal Office:	500 Rue St. Jacques 11th Flr.

Organization	Category	Mandate	Contact Information
			Montréal, QC H2Y 1S1 t: 514-289-8327 f: 514-289-0422
		Halifax Office:	1785 Barrington St. P.O. Box 427 Halifax, NS t: 902-420-8530 f: 902-420-8061
		Vancouver Office:	Toronto Dominion Tower Branch 700 West Georgia Vancouver, BC V7Y 1A2 t: 604-654-3513 f: 604-654-3489

Foreign Broadcasters

Organization	Category	Mandate	Contact Information
Australia			
ABC Australia	National Broadcaster	Broadcasting a wide genre of programming from news to documentary, to children's programming,	Australian Broadcasting Corporation 700 Harris St. Ultimo 2007 GPO Box 9994 Sydney, NSW 2001 Australia www.abc.net.au t: +61 -2-9333-1500 f: +61 -2-9950-3055
Arena TV	Regional Cable Broadcaster	Broadcasting a wide mix of entertainment-based programming.	P.O. Box 2692 Sydney, NSW 1044 Australia t: +61-2-9200-1999 f: +61-2-9200-1097 www.arenatv.com.au
Australia Television	Regional Cable Broadcaster	Broadcasting a wide genre of programming from news to sports to drama and film.	221 Pacific Hwy Gore Hill 2065 Sydney, NSW 2001 Australia www.austv.com.au t: +61-2-9950-3090 f: +61-2-9950-3055
Discovery Channel Australia	National Cable Broadcaster	Programming on themes of nature, environment, science and technology,	117 Harris St. Pyromont Sydney, NSW 2009 Australia

Organization	Category	Mandate	Contact Information
		adventure, people and places. www. discovery.com/diginets/international/ ausnewzeal/ausnewzeal.html	t: +61-2-9552-1677 f: +61-2-9552-2029
Horizon Learning Channel	Regional Broadcaster	Broadcasting a mixture of educational and entertainment programming.	7 Martin St. South Melbourne Australia V1C 3205 t: +61-3-9699-7144 f: +61-3-9699-4947 www.ausmedia.com/horizon.htm
Lifestyle Channel	National Cable Channel	Mandate is to broad- cast lifestyle programming,	GPO Box 2693 Sydney NSW 1044 Australia t: +61-1902-220-300 f: +61-2-9200-1099 www.foxtel.com.au/perm/channels/19A.htm
National Geographic Channel Australia	National Cable Channel	Mandate is to broad- cast programming based on wildlife, people, culture, and educational programming.	Wharf 8 GPO Box 99 Pyrmont NSW 2009 Australia t: +61-2-9200-1234 f: +61-2-9200-1956 www.nationalgeographic.com.au
Nine Network	National Cable Channel	Broadcasting a wide genre of entertainment-based programming.	24 Artarmon Rd. P.O. Box 27 Willoughby NSW 2068 Australia t: +61-2-9906-9999 f: +61 -2-9958-2191

Organization	Category	Mandate	Contact Information
Odyssey TV	National Cable Channel	Broadcasting high quality documentary programming.	50 Yeo St. P.O. Box 94 Neutral Bay NSW 2089 Australia t: +61-2-9904-3333 f: +61-2-9904-3520 www.odysseytelevision.com
Ten Network	National Cable Channel	Broadcasting a wide genre of entertainment programming.	Saunders St. Pyrmont NSW 20091 Australia t: +61-2-9650-1010 f: +61-2-9650-1005 www.ten.com.au
The Comedy Channel Australia	National Cable Channel	Mandate is to broadcast programming of a comedic nature.	Wharf 8 Pyrmont NSW 2009 Australia t: +61-2-9200-1234 f: +61-2-9200-1244 www. thecomedychannel.com.au
TV1	National Cable Channel	Broadcasting a wide genre of entertainment programming.	55 Pyrmont Bridge Pyrmont NSW 2009 Australia t: +61-2-9976-2783 f: +61-2-9776-2537 www.tv1.com.au

Organization	Category	Mandate	Contact Information
New Zealand			
TV NZ New Zealand	National Broadcaster	Broadcasts a wide genre of entertainment programming.	100 Victoria St. W. P.O. Box 3819 Auckland New Zealand t: +64- 9-377- 0630/375-0790 f: +64-9-375-0593 www.tvnz.co.nz
TV3 New Zealand	National Broadcaster	Broadcasts a wide genre of entertainment programming.	3 Flower St. Eden Terrace Private Bag 92624 Symonds St. Auckland New Zealand t: +64-9-377-9730 f: +64-9-302-2103 www.tv3.co.nz
Europe			
Austria			
ORF1 & ORF 2	National Public Broadcaster	Broadcasts a wide range of programming from documentaries to arts and news.	Wurzburggasse 30 1136 Wien Austria t: +43 1 8787 80 f: +43 1 8787 82250 www.orf.at

Organization	Category	Mandate	Contact Information
Belgium			
BRTN TV1 & TV2	National Public Broadcaster	Broadcasts a range of programming from documentaries to arts and news, a portion of which is in the Flemish language.	Reyerslaan 52 1043 Bruxelles, Belgium t: +32-2-741-31-11 f: +32-2-734-93-51 www.brtn.be
Canal + Belgique	National Cable Broadcaster	Broadcasts a wide range of entertainment programming in the French language.	Chaussée de Louvain 656 1030 Bruxelles Belgium t: +32-2-730-02-11 f: +32-2-732-18-48 www.cplus.be
RTBF	National Public Broadcaster	Broadcasts a wide range of programming from arts to education and entertainment in the French language.	Cité Reyers 1044 Bruxelles Belgium t: +32-2-737-21-11 f: +32-2-737-42-44 www.rtbf.be
Denmark			
DR TV Danish Broadcasting Corporation	National Public Broadcaster	Broadcasts a wide range of programming from arts and documentaries, to entertainment.	DR 1 Mörkhöjvej 500 2860 Söborg Denmark t: +45-35-203-040 f: +45-35-204-100/ www.dr.dk

Organization	Category	Mandate	Contact Information
TV2	National Public Broadcaster	Broadcasts a wide range of programming from arts and documentaries, to entertainment.	Rugaardsvej 25 5100 Odense Denmark t: 45 65 91 91 91 f: 45 65 91 85 14
TV3	National Public Broadcaster	Broadcasts a wide range of programming from arts and documentaries, to entertainment.	Indiakaj 6 2100 Kobenhavn Denmark t: 45 35 25 90 00 f: 45 35 25 90 10
Finland			
Canal + Finland	National Cable Broadcaster	Broadcasts a wide range of entertainment programming.	PL 66 Helsinki 00581 Finland t: +358-203-22625 www.canalplus.fi
MTV3	National Private Broadcaster	Broadcasts a wide range of entertainment programming.	Ilmalantori 2 00033 MTV3 Finland t: +358 -9-15-001 f: +358- 9-15-007-07 www.mtv3.fi
TV Finland (YLE FST Finland; YLE TV1 &	National Public Broadcaster	Broadcasts a wide range of programming from children's	Radiokatu 5 Box 80 00024 Ylesradio Finland

Organization	Category	Mandate	Contact Information
YLE TV2)		programs, to news, documentaries and entertainment. www.yle.fi/fbc/television/tvfinland.html	t: +358-9-1480-3537 f: +358-9-1480-3388
France			
ARTE	National Cable Channel French-German Broadcaster	Broadcasts a wide range of entertainment programs in the German and French languages.	ARTE 2 a, rue de la Fonderie 67080 Strasbourg Cedex France t: +33-3-88-14-22-22 f: +33-3-88-14-22-20 www.lasept-arte.fr ARTE G.E.I.E. 2 a, rue de la Fonderie 67080 Strasbourg Cedex France t: +33-3-88-14-22-22 f: +33-3-88-14-22-20 www.arte-tv.com
Canal J	National Cable Channel	Specialty broadcaster for children and youth programming.	91, bis rue du Cherche-Midi 75286 Paris Cedex 06 France t: 33-1-49-54-54-54 f: 33-1-42-22-87-17 www.canalj.fr

Organization	Category	Mandate	Contact Information
Canal Jimmy	National Cable Channel	Broadcasts a wide range of entertainment programming.	42 quai du Point du Jour Boulogne Billancourt 92100 France t: +33-1-46-10-10-10 f: +33-1-47-61-94-00 www.canal-jimmy.tm.fr
Canal +	National Cable Channel	Broadcasts a wide range of entertainment programming.	85/89 quai André Citroen 75711 Paris Cedex 15 France t: +33-1-49-87-27-27 f: +33-1-44-25-12-34
Canal + Horizons	National Cable Channel	Broadcasts a wide range of entertainment programming.	101 rue Leblanc 75015 Paris France t: +33-1-40-60-39-00 f: +33-1-40-60-70-23 www.canalhorizons.com
France 2	National Public Broadcaster	Programming that covers all genres including news, sports, documentaries, entertainment and children's programming.	7 Esplanade Henri de France Maison de France Télévision 75907 Paris Cedex 15 France t: +33-1-56-22-42-42 f: +33-1-44-21-51-45 www.france2.fr
France 3	National Public Broadcaster	Programming that covers all genres	7 Esplanade Henri de France

Organization	Category	Mandate	Contact Information
		including news, sports, documentaries, entertainment and children's programming.	Maison de France Télévision 75907 Paris Cedex 15 France t: +33-1-56-22-30-30 f: +33-1-56-22-68-03 www.france3.fr
La Cinquième	National Public Broadcaster	Broadcasts a wide range of entertainment programming.	10-12 rue Hornace Vernet 92136 Issy-les-Moulineaux Cedex France t: +33-1-41-46-56-51 f: +33-1-41-46-54-33 www.lacinquieme.fr
La Chaîne Histoire (TPS)	National Cable Channel	Broadcasts a wide range of entertainment programming.	19 rue Cognacq-Jay 75007 Paris France t: +33-1-40-62-79-89 f: +33-1-40-62-19-00 www.histoire.fr
Mezzo (TPS)	National Cable Broadcaster	Programming dedicated to arts and culture.	49 blvd. Du Général Martial Valin 75015 Paris France t: +33-1-53-98-23-18 f: +33-1-53-98-23-01 www.mezzo.fr
Muzzik	National Cable Broadcaster	Programming dedicated to arts and	109 rue du Faubourg St-Honoré

Organization	Category	Mandate	Contact Information
		culture.	75008 Paris France t: +33-1-53-89-06-60 f: +33-1-53-89-06-67 www.muzzik.fr
Odyssée (TPS) La Chaine Documentaire	National Cable Broadcaster	Programming dedicated to the documentary form.	145 quai de Stalingrad 92137 Issy-les-Moulineaux Cedex France t: +33-1-41-33-86-10 f: +33-1-41-33-86-11
Planète (CSN)	National Cable Broadcaster	Specialty channel broadcasting factual programmes and documentaries.	BP 2009 25 rue Leblanc 92518 Boulogne Billancourt Cedex Paris, France t: +33-1-46-10-10-10 f: +33-1-47-61-94-00 www.planete-cable.tm.fr
Télétoon (TPS)	National Cable Broadcaster	Broadcasts a wide range of entertainment programming.	145 quai de Stalingrad 92137 Issy-les-Moulineaux Cedex France t: +33-1-41-33-89-93 f: +33-1-41-33-89-80 www.tps.fr/Services/Chaines/TeleToon.htm

Organization	Category	Mandate	Contact Information
Téva (TPS)	National Cable Broadcaster	Programming of interest to women.	89 ave. Charles de Gaulle 92575 Neuilly-sur Seine Cedex Paris, France t: +33-1-41-92-68-81 f: +33-1-41-92-68-89 www.tps.fr/Services/Chaines/Teva.htm
TF1	National Cable Broadcaster	Broadcasting a wide range of entertainment programs.	1 quai du Point du Jour 92656 Boulogne Billancourt Cedex Paris, France t: +33-1-41-41-27-32 t: +33-1-41-41-12-34 f: +33-1-41-41-29-10 www.tf1.fr
TV5	National Cable Channel	Broadcasting a wide genre of programming from news, to documentaries, to entertainment.	19 rue Cognacq-Jay 75007 Paris France t: +33-1-44-18-55-55 f: +33-1-44-18-55-10 www.tv5.org/europe
Voyage (CSN)	National Cable Channel	Programming dedicated to travel.	2 rue Rouget del'isle 92130 Issy-les-Moulineaux France t: +33-1-41-33-31-31 f: +33-1-41-33-31-18 www.voyage.fr

Organization	Category	Mandate	Contact Information
Germany			
ARD Das Erste	Regional Broadcaster	Broadcasting depicts a wide range of options from documentaries, to culture, to children's programming.	Arnulfstraße 42 Programm-information D-80335 Munich Germany t: +49-89-5900-3869 f: +49-89-5900-3880 www.das-erste.de
ARD/BR3 Bayern 3	Regional Broadcaster	Broadcasting depicts a wide range of options from documentaries, to culture, to children's programming.	Rundfunkplatz 1 D-80300 Munich Germany t: +49-89-5900-01 f: +49-89-5900-2375 www.br-online.de
ARD/HR Hessischer Rundfunk	Regional Broadcaster	Broadcasting depicts a wide range of options from documentaries, to culture, to children's programming.	Bertramstraße 8 60320 Frankfurt /Main Germany t: +49-69-155-1 f: +49-69-155-2900 www.hr-online.de
ARD/MDR Mittel-deutscher Rundfunk	Regional Broadcaster	Broadcasting depicts a wide range of options from documentaries, to culture, to children's programming.	Kantstrasse 71-73 04275 Leipzig Germany t: +49-341-30-00 f: +49-341-300-5544 www.mdr.de

Organization	Category	Mandate	Contact Information
ARD/NDR	Regional Broadcaster	Broadcasting depicts a wide range of options from documentaries, to culture, to children's programming.	Rothenbaum-chaussee 132 20149 Hamburg Germany t: +49-40-415-6-0 f: +49-40-447-602 www.ndr.de
ARD/ORB Ostdeutscher Rundfunk Brandenburg	Regional Broadcaster	Broadcasting depicts a wide range of options from documentaries, to culture, to children's programming.	August-Bebel-Strasse 26-53 14482 Potsdam-Babelsberg Germany t: +49-331-731-0 f: +49-331-721-3571 www.orb.de
ARD/RB Radio Bremen	Regional Broadcaster	Broadcasting depicts a wide range of options from documentaries, to culture, to children's programming.	Hans-Bredow-strasse 10 28353 Bremen Germany t: +49-421-246-0 f: +49-421-246-2029 www.radiobremen.de
ARD/SFB Sender Freies Berlin	Regional Broadcaster	Broadcasting depicts a wide range of options from documentaries, to culture, to children's programming.	Masurenallee 8-14 14057 Berlin Germany t: +49-30-3031-0 f: +49-30-301-5062 www.sfb.de
ARD/SR Saarländischer	Regional Broadcaster	Broadcasting depicts a wide range of	Funkhaus Halberg 66100 Saarbrücken

Organization	Category	Mandate	Contact Information
Rundfunk		options from documentaries, to culture, to children's programming.	Germany t: +49-681-602-0 f: +49-681-602-3874 www.sr-online.de
ARD/SWR Südwest Rundfunk	Regional Broadcaster	Broadcasting depicts a wide range of options from documentaries, to culture, to children's programming.	Regional Offices:
		Baden Baden Office:	Funkhaus Baden-Baden Hans-BredowStraße 76530 Baden Baden Germany t: +49-722-192-0 f: +49-722-192-2010 www.sur-online.de
		Stuttgart Office:	Funkaus Stuttgart Neckarstraße 230 70190 Stuttgart t: +49-71-1929-0
		Mainz Office:	Funkhaus Mainz Am Fort Gonsenheim 39 55122 Mainz Germany t: +49-613-1929-0

Organization	Category	Mandate	Contact Information
ARD/WDR Westdeutscher Rundfunk	Regional Broadcaster	Broadcasting depicts a wide range of options from documentaries, to culture, to children's programming.	Appellhofplatz 1 50667 Köln Germany t: +49-221-220-1 f: +49-221-220-4800 www.wdr.de
ARTE Deutschland	National Cable Broadcaster	Broadcasts a wide range of entertainment programming.	Arte Deutschland TV GmbH Schützenstraße 1 76530 Baden Baden Germany t: +49-72-21-9369-0 f: +49-72-21-9369-50 www.arte-tv.com
3sat	Regional Broadcaster	Programming dedicated to culture and information.	ARD Koordination 3SAT Hans Bredow Stn. 76522 Baden Baden Germany t: +49-72-2192-2914 f: +49-72-2192-2174 www.3sat.de
DW Deutsche Welle	Regional Broadcaster	Broadcasts a wide range of entertainment programming.	50968 Köln Raderberggürtel 50 Germany t: +49-221-389-0 f: +49-221-389-3000 www.dwelle.de
MDR Mittel	National Broadcaster	Broadcasts a wide range of	Kanstrabe 71-73 04275 Leipzig

Organization	Category	Mandate	Contact Information
Deutscher Rundfink		entertainment and information programming.	Hans 8 t: +49-300-7207 f: +49-300-7281 www.mdr.de
Premiere	Regional Broadcaster	Broadcasts a wide range of entertainment programming.	Tonndorfer Hauptstrasse 90 22045 Hamburg Germany t: +49-40-6680-0 f: +49-40-6680-1199 www.premiere.de
Pro Sieben	National Broadcaster	Broadcasts a wide range of entertainment programming.	Medienallee 7 85767 Unterfoehring Germany t: +89 95 07 12 07 f: +89 95 07 12 11 www.pro-sieben.com
RTL 2	National Broadcaster	Broadcasts a wide range of entertainment programming.	Bavariafilmplatz 7 82031 Gruenwald Germany t: +89-64-185-211 f: +89-64-185-219 www.rtl.de
Telepool	Regional Broadcaster	Broadcasts a wide range of entertainment programming.	*Headquarters:* Sonnenstrasse 21 D-80331 Munich Germany t: +49-89-558-760 f: +49-89-558-7618-8 www.telepoolgmbh.com

Organization	Category	Mandate	Contact Information
ZDF Zweites Deutsches Fernsehen	Regional Broadcaster	Broadcasts a wide range of entertainment programming. *Hanover:*	*Wiesbaden:* Unter den Eichen 5 65195 Wiesbaden Germany t: +49-611-590-544 f: +49-611-520-853 Auf dem Emmerberge 23 30169 Hannover Germany t: +49-511-9882-041 f: +49-511-801-131
Ireland			
BBC1 Northern Ireland	Regional Public Broadcaster	Programming that covers all genres including news, sports, documentaries, entertainment and children's programming.	Broadcasting House Ormeau Avenue Belfast BT2 8HQ t: +44-1232-338-224 f: +44-1232-326-453 www.bbc.co.uk/northernireland
RTÉ 1 & Network 2	National Public Broadcaster	Programming that covers all genres including news, sports, documentaries, entertainment and children's programming.	Donnybrook Dublin 4 Ireland t: +353-1-208-3111 f: +353-1-208-3080 www.rte.ie/tv

Organization	Category	Mandate	Contact Information
Italy			
Canale 5	Regional Broadcaster	Broadcasts a wide range of entertainment programming.	Viale Europa 48 Cologno Monzese It-20093 Milano, Italy t: +39-2-2514-7524 f: +39-2-2514-9162 www.canale5.com
Italia 1	Regional Broadcaster	Broadcasts a wide range of entertainment programming.	Palazzo del Cigni Segrate 20090 It-20137 Milano, Italy t: +39-2-2514-9183 www.italia1.com
RAI Uno	National Public Broadcaster	Programming that covers all genres including news, sports, documentaries, entertainment and children's programming.	Viale Mazzini 14 It-00100 Roma, Italy t: +39-6-3878-1/3861 f: +39-6-372-5680 www.raiuno.rai.it
RAI Due	National Public Broadcaster	Programming that covers all genres including news, sports, documentaries, entertainment and children's programming.	Viale Mazzini 14 It-00195 Roma, Italy t: +39-6-3878-1/3861 f: +39-6-372-5680 www.rai.it/raidue.html

Organization	Category	Mandate	Contact Information
RAI Tre	National Public Broadcaster	Programming that covers all genres including news, sports, documentaries, entertainment and children's programming.	Viale Mazzini 14 It-00195 Roma, Italy t: +39-6-3878-1 f: +39-6-372-5680 www.rai.it/raitre.html
Norway			
Canale + Norway	Regional Broadcaster	Broadcasts a wide range of entertainment programming.	Brynsvn.13 Postboks 80 Bryn N-0611, Oslo Norway t: +47-22-93-93-33 www.canalplus.no
NRK1	Regional Broadcaster	Programming that covers all genres including news, sports, documentaries, entertainment and children's programming.	Bjorstjerne Bjornsons plass 1 340 Oslo Norway t: +47-23-04-70-00 f: +47-23-04-98-33 www.nrk.no/nrk1
NRK2	Regional Broadcaster	Programming that covers all genres including news, sports, documentaries, entertainment and children's programming.	Bjorstjerne Bjornsons plass 1 340 Oslo Norway t: +47-23-04-70-00 f: +47-23-04-74-80 www.nrk.no/nrk2

Organization	Category	Mandate	Contact Information
TV Norge	National Public Broadcaster	Broadcasting a wide range of entertainment programming.	Sagveien 17 0458 Oslo Norway t: +47-22-387-800 f: +47-22-051-000 www.tvnorge.no
TV2 Norway	National Broadcaster	Programming that covers all genres including news, sports, documentaries, entertainment and children's programming.	Postboks 2 Nöstegt.72 N-5002 Bergen Norway t: +47-55-90-80-70 f: +47-55-90-80-90 www.tv2.no
TV3 Norge	National Cable Broadcaster	Broadcasts a wide range of entertainment programming.	Postboks TV3 Youngstorget N-0028 Oslo Norway t: +47-22-99-00-33 f: +47-22-99-00-93/18 www.tv3.no
Spain			
Andalucía TV	Regional Broadcaster	Broadcasts a wide range of entertainment programming.	ctra. San Juan de Aznalfarache Apartado de Correos 132 41920 San Juan de Aznalfarache (Seville) Spain t: +34-95-560-7600 f: +34-95-60-7799 www.canalsur.es

Organization	Category	Mandate	Contact Information
Canal + Espana (Cal Sur)	Regional Broadcaster	Broadcasts a wide range of entertainment programming.	Apartado de correos 4900 ES-28087 Madrid Spain t: +34-91-304-15-15 f: +34-91-396-57-90 www.cplus.es
CCV Canal Comunitat Valenciana (Canal 9 TVV)	Regional Broadcaster	Programming that covers all genres including news, sports documentaries, entertainment and children's programming.	Polígon Accés Ademuz s/n 46100 Burjassot Valencia Spain t: +34-96-318-30-00 f: +34-96-318-31-55 www.rtvv.es
ETB (Euskal Telebista) (ETB 1 & ETB 2)	Regional Broadcaster	Broadcasts a wide range of entertainment programming in the Basque language.	Iurreta s/n 48200 Bizkaia Spain t: +34-94-620-3000 f: +34-94-620-0681 www.eitb.com
TVE 1 & TVE 2	Regional Broadcaster	Programming that covers all genres including news, sports, documentaries, entertainment and children's programming.	c/Alcade Saénz de Baranda, 92 28036 Madrid Spain t: +34-91-346-4000 f: +34-91-346-8553 +34-91-346-8559 www.rtve.es/tve
TV 3 Televisíon de Catalunya	Regional Broadcaster	Programming that covers all genres including news,	carrer de la TV3 s/n 08970 Sant Joan Despi, Spain

Organization	Category	Mandate	Contact Information
(TV3 & Canal 33)		sports, documentaries, entertainment and children's programming.	t: +34-93-499-9333 f: +34-93-473-0671 www.tvc.es
TVG Spain Companía de Radio-Televisíon de Galicia	Regional Broadcaster	Programming that covers all genres including news, sports, documentaries, entertainment and children's programming.	Apartado 707 San Marcos 15820 Santiago de Compostela La Coruna Spain t: +34-981-540-737 f: +34-981-540-719 www.crtvg.es
Sweden			
Canal + Sweden	Regional Broadcaster	Broadcasts a wide range of entertainment programming.	Tegeluddvägen 7 115 84 Stockholm Sweden t: +46-8-459-2800 f: +46-8-459-2801 www.canalplus.se
Kanal 5 Sweden	Regional Broadcaster	Broadcasts a wide range of entertainment programming.	Brunbärsvägen 7 11499 Stockholm Sweden t: +46-8-674-1500 f: +46-8-612-57-30 www.kanal5.se
SVT1 & SVT2 (SVT Sweden)	Regional Broadcaster	Programming that covers all genres including news, sports,	Oxenstiernsgatan 26-34 105 10 Stockholm

Organization	Category	Mandate	Contact Information
		documentaries, entertainment and childrens programming.	Sweden t: +46-8-784-0000 f: +46-8-784-1500 www.svt.e
TV3 Sweden	Regional Broadcaster	Broadcasts a wide range of entertainment programming.	P.O. Box 210 52 100 31 Stockholm Sweden t: +46-8-5620-2300 f: +46-8-5620-3330 www.tv3.se
TV4 Sweden	Regional Broadcaster	Broadcasts a wide range of entertainment programming.	Tegeluddsvagen 5 11 579 Stockholm Sweden t: +46-8-459-4000 f: +46-8-459-4444 www.tv4.se
Switzerland			
SF1 (DRS)	Regional Broadcaster	Broadcasts a wide range of entertainment programming.	Fernsehstrasse 1-4 8052, Zürich Switzerland t: +41-1-305-6611 f: +41-1-305-5660 www.sfdrs.
SF2 (Schweiz 4)	Regional Broadcaster	Broadcasts a wide range of entertainment programming.	Fernsehstrasse 1-4 8052 Zürich Switzerland t: +41-1- 3056611 f: +41-1- 305-5660 www.sfdrs.ch

Organization	Category	Mandate	Contact Information
TS1 Switzerland	Regional Broadcaster	Programming that covers all genres including news, sports, documentaries, entertainment and children's programming.	Tele Suisse Italianne Casella Postale 6903 Lugano-Besso Switzerland t: +41-91-803-5803 f: +41-91-803-5575 www.rtsi.ch/tsi
TSR Switzerland	Regional Broadcaster	Programming that covers all genres including news, sports, documentaries, entertainment and children's programming.	Télévision Suisse Romande 20 quai Ernest Ansermet Case postale 234 1205 Geneva Switzerland t: +41-22-708-9911 f: +41-22-781-1908 www.tsr.ch
The Netherlands			
AVRO The Netherlands	National Public Broadcaster	Specializing in arts and culture programming.	Postbus 2 1200 JA Hilversum Netherlands t: +31-35-671-7911 f: +31-35-671-7443 www.omroep.nl/avro
EO The Netherlands (Evangelical Broadcasting Corporation)	Regional Broadcaster	Specializing in documentaries and stories of faith.	P.O. Box 21000 1202 BB Hilversum Netherlands t: +31-35-647-4770 f: +31-35-647-4544 www.omroep.nl/eo/foreign

Organization	Category	Mandate	Contact Information
IKON	National Public Broadcaster	Specializing in documentary programming.	Postbus 10009 1201 DA Hilversum Netherlands t: +31-35-672-7272 f: +31-35-621-5100 www.omroep.nl/ikone:ikon@ikon.nl
Nederland TV1	Regional Broadcaster	Broadcasts a wide range of entertainment programming.	NOS Nederlandse Omroep Stichting P.O. Box 26444 1202 JJ Hilversum Netherlands t: +31-35-677-3561/8039 f: +31-35-677-5318 www.nos.nl
RTL4 & RTL5	Regional Broadcaster	Broadcasts a wide range of entertainment programming.	Franciscusweg 219 Postbus 15000 1216 SE Hilversum Netherlands t: +31-35-671-8711 f: +31-35-623-6892 www.rtl4.nl
RVU Educatieve Omroep (RVU) (Educational Network)	National Broadcaster	Specializing in educational programming.	RVU Educatieve Omroep Postbus 1950 1200 BZ Hilversum Netherlands t: +31-35-624-0551 f: +31-35-624-0555 www.omroep.nl/rvu

Organization	Category	Mandate	Contact Information
SBS 6	National Cable Broadcaster	Broadcasting a wide range of entertainment programming.	Plantage Middenlaan 14 Postbus 18179 1001 ZB Amsterdam Netherlands t: +31-20-522-5555 f: +31-20-522-5556 www.sb6.nl
United Kingdom			
BBC 1 & 2	National Public Broadcaster	Programming that covers all genres including news, sports, documentaries, entertainment and children's programming.	BBC Television Centre Wood Lane London W12 7RJ UK t: +44-181-743-8000 www.bbc.co.uk (CONTACT INDIVIDUAL DEPARTMENTS FOR FAX NUMBERS.)
BBC Knowledge	National Broadcaster	Programming centred on educational aspects.	Television Centre Wood Lane London W12 7RJ UK t: +44-181-743-8000 f: +44-208-752-7645 www.bbc. co.uk/knowledge
BBC Midlands	Regional Public Broadcaster	Programming that covers all genres including news, sports, documentaries	Pebble Mill Road Birmingham B57QQ UK

Organization	Category	Mandate	Contact Information
		entertainment and children's programming.	t: +44 121 414 8888￼ f: +44 121 414 8634￼ www.bbc.co.uk
BBC North	Regional Public Broadcaster	Programming that covers all genres including news, sports, documentaries, entertainment and children's programming.	New Broadcasting House￼ Oxford Rd.￼ Manchester￼ M60 1SJ￼ UK￼ t: +44 161200 2020￼ f: +44 161 236 1005￼ www.bbc.co.uk
BBC1 Scotland	National Public Broadcaster	Programming that covers all genres including news, sports, documentaries, entertainment and children's programming.	Broadcasting House￼ Queen Margaret Dr.￼ Glasgow￼ G12 8DG￼ Scotland￼ t: +44 141 339 8844￼ f: +44 141 338 2792￼￼ www.bbc.co.uk/scotland
BBC South	Regional Public Broadcaster	Programming that covers all genres including news, sports, documentaries, entertainment and children's programming.	Broadcasting House￼ Whitladies Road￼ Bristol￼ BS8 2LR￼ UK￼ t: +44 117 973 2211￼ f: +44 117 923 7934￼ www.bbc.co.uk
BBC Wales	Regional Public Broadcaster	Programming that covers all genres including news, sports,	Broadcasting House￼ Llandaff￼ Cardiff

Organization	Category	Mandate	Contact Information
		documentaries, entertainment and children's programming.	CF5 2YQ UK t: +44-1222-322-000 f: +44-208-752-7645 www.bbc.co.uk/wales/tv
BBC Prime	Regional Broadcaster	Programming evolving around comedy, natural history, children's and educational programmes.	BBC Prime 80 Wood Lane Woodlands London W12 0TT UK t: +44-181-576-2000 f: +44-181-576-3040 www.bbcprime.comB
Carlton Television	Regional Broadcaster	Programming that covers all genres including news, sports, documentaries, entertainment and children's programming.	101 St. Martin's Lane London WC2N 4AZ UK t: +44-171-240-4000 f: +44-171-240-4171 www.carltonselect.co.uk
Channel 4	National Public Broadcaster	Broadcasting a wide range of entertainment programming.	124 Horseferry Rd. London SW1P 2TX UK t: +44-171-396-4444 f: +44-171-306-8356 www. channel4.co.uk
Channel 5	National Broadcaster	Broadcasting a wide range of	22 Long Acre London

Organization	Category	Mandate	Contact Information
		entertainment programming.	WC2E 9LY UK t: +44-171-550-5555 f: +44-171-550-5554 www.channel5.co.uk
Discovery U.K.	Specialty Cable Channel	Specializing in science, technology, natural history, archeology and anthropology programming. www.discovery.com/diginets/international/europe/europe.html	P.O. Box 846 Bristol BS99 5HR UK t: +44-117-909-1221 f: +44-117-925-3525
Grampian Television	Regional Broadcaster	Broadcasting a wide range of entertainment programming. www.scottish mediagroup.com/broadcasting/gtv.html	Queen's Cross Aberdeen AB15 4XJ Scotland t: +44-1224-846-846 f: +44-1224-846-800
Granada	Regional Broadcaster	Broadcasting a wide range of entertainment programming.	Quay St. Manchester M60 9EA UK t: +44-161-832-7211 f: +44-161-953-0283 www.granadatv.co.uk
The History Channel	National Cable Channel	Specializing in programming of a	British Sky Broadcasting Ltd.

Organization	Category	Mandate	Contact Information
		historical nature.	Grant Way Isleworth, Middlesex TW7 5QD UK t: +44-171-705-3000 f: +44-171-707-3030 www.sky.co.uk/history/index.htm
ITV	Regional Broadcaster	Programming that covers all genres including news, sports, documentaries, entertainment and children's programming.	ITV Network Centre 200 Gray's Inn Rd. London WC1X 8HF UK t: +44-171-843-8000 f: +44-171-843-8158 www.itv.co.uk
S2, Scottish Media Group	Regional Broadcaster	Broadcasting a wide range of entertainment programming.	S2, Scottish Media Group Cowcaddens Glasgow G2 3PR Scotland t: +44-141-300-3000 f: +44-141-300-3030 www.s2.co.uk
S4C Welsh Fourth Channel	Regional Public Broadcaster	Programming that covers all genres including news, sports, documentaries, entertainment and children's programming.	Parc Ty Glas Llanishen Cardiff CF4 5DU Scotland t: +44-1222-747-444 f: +44-1222-754-444 www.s4c.co.uk

Organization	Category	Mandate	Contact Information
Scottish Television	Regional Broadcaster	Programming that covers all genres including news, sports, documentaries, entertainment and children's programming.	Scottish Television Cowcaddens Glasgow G2 3PR Scotland t: +44-141-300-3000 f: +44-141-300-3030 www.scottishmediagroup.com/ broadcasting/stv.html
Sky Travel	Regional Broadcaster	Programming centred around travel.	British Sky Broadcasting Grant Way Isleworth, Middlesex TW7 5QD UK t: +44-171-705-3000 f: +44-171-705-3030 www.sky.co.uk
The Travel Channel	Regional Broadcaster	Specializing in travel documentaries.	66 Newman St. London W1P 3LA UK t: +44-171-636-5401 f: +44-171-636-6424
UTV	Regional Broadcaster in Ireland	Broadcasts a wide range of entertainment programming.	Havelock House Ormeau Rd. Belfast BT7 1EB Ireland t: +44-1232-328-122 f: +44-1232-246-695 www.utvlive.com

American Broadcasters

Organization	Category	Mandate	Contact Information
A & E	National Cable Broadcaster	Specializing in documentary and entertainment programming.	A & E Television Networks 235 East. 45th St. New York, NY USA 10017 t: 212-210-1340 f: 212-210-9755 www.aetv.com
ACCESS	National Cable Broadcaster	Broadcasts a wide range of entertainment programming.	2600 Michelson Dr. #1650 Irvine, CA 92612 USA t: 949-263-9900 f: 949-757-1526 www.accesstv.com
AIN American Independent Network	National Cable Channel	Specializing in family oriented programming.	6125 Airport Freeway Ste. 200 Haltom City, TX USA 76117 t: 817-222-1234 f: 817-222-9809 www.aini.com
Animal Planet	National Cable Channel	Programming focused on animals and wildlife.	P.O. Box 665 Florence, KY USA 41022 t: 301-986-0444 f: 301-606-727-8918 www.animal.discovery.com

Organization	Category	Mandate	Contact Information
Bravo USA Channel	National Cable Channel	Specializing in arts and entertainment programming.	150 Crossways Park West Woodbury, NY USA 11797 t: 516-396-4500 f: 516-364-7638 www.bravotv.com
Discovery Channel USA	National Cable Broadcaster	Specializing in science, technology, anthropology and wildlife programming.	7700 Wisconsin Ave Bethesda, MD USA 20814 t: 8301-986-0444 f: 301-986-1889 www.discovery.com
FFC Fox Family Channel	National Cable Channel	Broadcasting family programming.	P.O. Box 2050 Virginia Beach, VA USA 23452 t: 757-459-6000 f: 754-459-6420 www.fox familychannel.com
Hallmark Entertainment Network	National Cable Broadcaster	Specializing in family programming.	6430 South Fiddlers' Green Circle Ste. 500 Englewood, CO USA 80111 t: 303-220-7990 f: 303-220-7660 www.hall marknetwork.com
HGTV Home & Garden	National Cable Channel	Specializing in programming related to home, gardens and	P.O. Box 50970 Knoxville, TN USA 37950

Organization	Category	Mandate	Contact Information
Television		decorating.	t: 423-694-2700 f: 423-531-8933 www.hgtv.com
The History Channel	National Cable Channel	Specializing in historical programming and documentaries.	A&E Television Network 235 East 45th St. New York, NY USA 10017 t: 212-210-1340 f: 212-983-4370 www.historychannel.com
ITVS Independent Television Service	National Public Broadcaster	Broadcasting a wide range of entertainment programming.	51 Federal St., Ste. 401 San Francisco, CA USA 94107 t: 415-356-8383 f: 415-356-8391
Knowledge TV USA	National Cable Broadcaster	Broadcasting a wide range of documentary and educational programming.	9697 E. Mineral Ave. Englewood, CO USA 80112 t: 303-792-3111 f: 303-792-5608
Lifetime	National Cable Broadcaster	Specializing in programming of interest to women.	World Wide Plaza 309 West 49th St. New York, NY USA 10019 t: 212-424-7000 f: 212-957-4110 www.lifetimetv.com

Organization	Category	Mandate	Contact Information
Nickelodeon	National Cable Channel	Specializing in children's and family programming.	MTV Networks, Inc 1515 Broadway New York, NY USA 10036 t: 212-258-7579 f: 212-846-4985 www.nick.com
Odyssey Channel	National Cable Channel	Specializing in documentary, drama, music and entertainment programming.	74 Trinity Place 9th Flr. New York, NY USA 10006 t: 212-964-1663 f: 212-964-5966 www.odysseychannel.com
OLN Outdoor Life Network	National Cable Channel	Programming about the great outdoors.	2 Stamford Plaza 281 Tresser Blvd. Stamford, CT USA 06901 t: 203-406-2500 f: 203-406-2530 www.greatoutdoors.com/tv/index.htm
Ovation The Arts Network	National Cable Channel	Specializing in arts and cultural programming.	201 North Union St. Ste. 210 Alexandria, VA USA 22314 t: 800-OVATION www.ovationtv.com
PBS Public Broadcasting Service	National Public Broadcaster	Broadcasting a wide range of educational and entertainment programming.	PBS Program Offerings 475 L'Enfant Plaza Washington, DC

Organization	Category	Mandate	Contact Information
			USA 20024 or Television Activities Office CPB 111-16th St. N.W. Washington, DC USA 20036 or 1320 Braddock Pl Alexandria, VA USA 22314 t: 703-739-5000 f: 703-739-0775 www.pbs.org
The Learning Channel (TLC)	National Cable Channel	Specializing in educational and entertainment programming.	7700 Wisconsin Bethesda, MD 20814-3579 USA t: 888-404-5969 or 301-986-0444 f: 301-986-9552
The Travel Channel	National Cable Broadcaster	Programming focused on travel and adventure.	7700 Wisconsin Ave. Bethesda MD 20814-3579 USA t: 888-404-5969 or 301-986-0444 f: 301-986-9552 www.travelchannel.com

Organization	Category	Mandate	Contact Information
Turner Network Television (TNT)	National Cable Broadcaster	Broadcasting a wide range of entertainment programming.	1010 Techwood Dr. NW Atlanta, GA USA 30318 t: 404-885-4538 f: 404-885-0172 www.tnt-turner.com www.turner.com

Chapter Nine

Resource Materials Guide

There are several resource books that will help you raise financing for television as well as provide explanations on the business side of television. Below is a list of the resource books I recommend.

Art of the Deal. Published by PACT-Producers Alliance for Cinema & Television, 1997. London, UK. Contains sources of U.K. production financing as well as an overview of dealing with North American and International Broadcasters, told from a British point of view.
Telephone: +44-171-331-6000
Fax: +44-171-331-6700
Website: www.pact.co.uk

BFI Film and Television Handbook. Edited by Eddie Dyja. British Film Institute. Published Annually, London, UK. The essential reference guide to the U.K. film, television and video markets.
Telephone: +44 171 957 8919
Fax: +44 171 957 8920
Website: www.bfi.org.uk

BIB World Guide to Television. North American Publishing Company. Published Annually, Philadelphia, Pennsylvania. Reference guide to the international television industry.

Telephone: 888-484-5245
Fax: 215-283-5390
Website: www.bibnet.com

The Business of Television: A practical guide to the U.S. and International Television Industries. Howard J. Blumenthal and Oliver R. Goodenough. Published by Billboard Books, 1998. New York, New York. Practical guide to the business of television. Contains examples of television contracts as well as an explanation of how television is produced and distributed in North America and around the world.
Telephone: 212-764-7300
Fax: 212-536-5359

The Canadian Directory to Foundations. Canadian Centre for Philanthropy. Published Annually, Toronto, Ontario. Contains details of Canadian foundations who donate funds to arts and culture.
Telephone: 800-263-1178
Fax: 416-515-0773
Website: www.ccp.ca

Canadian Production Finance: A Producer's Handbook. Published by the Ontario Film Development Corporation, 1998. Toronto, Ontario. Includes samples of rights agreements, co-production agreements, recoupment schedules, budget cost report and distribution agreements.
Telephone: 416-314-6858
Fax: 416-314-6876

Contracts for the Film and Television Industry.
Mark Litwak. Silman-James Press, 1994. Los
Angeles, California. Examples of American
contracts which can be applied to the Canadian
film/television industry.
Telephone: 323-661-9922
Fax: 323-661-9933
Website: www.marklitwak.com

*Dealmaking in the Film and Television Industry: from
negotiations to final contracts.* Mark Litwak.
Silman-James Press, 1994. Los Angeles,
California. Contains information on how to deal
with television networks and film studios. Told
from an American point of view but makes
interesting reading.
Telephone: 323-661-9922
Fax: 323-661-9933
Website: www.marklitwak.com

Directory of Corporate Giving in Canada.
Rainforest Publications. Published Annually,
Nelson, British Columbia. Contains details of
organizations who donate funds to arts and
cultural activities.
Telephone: 800-655-7729
Fax: 902-894-2630
Website: www.iwave.com

European Documentary Network TV Guide.
European Documentary Network. Published
Annually, Denmark. Lists the European broadcasters who purchase documentaries from
independent producers.

Telephone: +45 33 13 11 22;
Fax: +45 33 13 11 44
Website: www.dox.dk

European Documentary Profiles and Film Funds.
European Documentary Network.   Published
Annually, Denmark. Lists the European broad-
casters who purchase documentaries and films
from independent producers; companion guide
to European Documentary Network TV Guide.
Telephone: +45 33 13 11 22
Fax: +45 33 13 11 44
Website: www.dox.dk

Film and Video Budgets, 2nd edition.   Michael
Wiese and Deke Simon. Published by Michael
Wiese Productions, 1995. Studio City, California.
Information on how to create film and video
budgets.
Telephone: 800-379-8808
Fax: 818-986-3408
Website: www.mwp.com

Film and Video Financing.   Michael Wiese.
Published by Michael Wiese Productions, 1991.
Studio City, California.   Advice on how to
finance film and video productions, told from an
American point of view.
Telephone: 800-379-8808
Fax: 818-986-3408
Website: www.mwp.com

Film and Video Marketing. Michael Wiese.
Published by Michael Wiese Productions, 1989.
Studio City, California. Information on how to

sell and distribute finished film and television productions, told from an American point of view.
Telephone: 800-379-8808
Fax: 818-986-3408
Website: www.mwp.com.

Guide to Canadian & US Documentary Buyers. Published by the Canadian Independent Film Caucus, 1998. Toronto, Ontario. Lists names and contact information for North American broadcasters who purchase documentaries.
Telephone: 416-599-3844
Fax: 416-656-8259

Guide to Canadian Arts Grants. Canada Grants Service. Published Annually, Toronto, Ontario. Lists government and private sources of financial assistance for the arts.
Telephone: 800-464-2048
Fax: 416-431-4695
Website: www.interlog.com/~cgs

The Guide: a practical guide to Canada's film television & multimedia industry. Canadian Film & Television Production Association. Published Annually, Toronto, Ontario. Reference guide to production companies, broadcasters, distributors and other useful information.
Telephone: 800-267-8208
Fax: 416-304-0499
Website: www.cftpa.ca

Home Video: Producing for the Home Market. Michael Wiese. Published by Michael Wiese

Film/Video, 1986. Studio City, California. Explains how to make video productions directed to individual consumers rather than broadcasters.
Telephone: 800-379-8808
Fax: 818-986-3408
Website: www.mwp.com

International Television Co-Production: From Access to Success. Carla B. Johnston. Focal Press is an imprint of Butterworth-Heinemann a division of Reed Publishing, 1992. Stoneham, Minnesota. Explains the legal and technical challenges of international co-productions.
Telephone: 781-904-2500
Fax: 781-933-6333
Website: www.bh.com

Making It: The Business of Film and Television Production in Canada. Barbara Hehner and Andra Sheffer Eds. The Academy of Canadian Cinema and Television. Published by Doubleday Canada Limited, 1995. Toronto, Ontario. Explains the overall process of making television and film productions from development to production to post-production and distribution.
Telephone: 416-977-7891
Fax: 416-977-8707

Marketing for Dummies. Alexander Haim. Published by IDG Books Worldwide, 1997. Foster City, California. Provides clear-cut details on how to market a business and a product, can be applied to any situation.
Telephone: 800-762-2974

Fax: 416-923-4821
Website: www.dummies.com

Matthews Media Directory. Canadian Corporate News. Published Bi-Annually, Toronto, Ontario. Comprehensive guide which lists all the media outlets including television in Canada and provides detailed descriptions on ownership as well as names of Programming Directors.
Telephone: 800-363-9296
Fax: 416-955-0705
Website: www.cdn-news.com

The Media Guide. Edited by Steve Peak and Paul Fisher. Published by Fourth Estate Ltd., Guardian News Service Ltd. Published Annually, London, UK. Lists television stations, cable, radio, newspapers and various media information in the U.K.
Telephone: +44 171 727 8993
Fax: +44 171 792 3176
Website: www.mediauk.com

The On-Production Budget Book. Robert J. Koster. Focal Press is an imprint of Butterworth-Heinemann, 1997. Newton, Massachusetts. Offers novices and experienced producers advice on how to create production budgets.
Telephone: 617-928-2500
Fax: 617-928-2620
Website: www.bh.com/focalpress

Producers Workbook III. Published by Vancouver Women in Film & Video, 1999. Vancouver, BC. Provides examples of contracts, budgets and

general information for producers.
Telephone: 604-685-1152
Fax: 604-685-1124
web: www.canadafilm.com/wifvv

Shaking the Money Tree: How to get grants and donations for film and video. Morrie Warshawski. Published by Michael Wiese Productions, 1994. Studio City, California. Details how to successfully achieve grants and donations for film and video, told from an American point of view.
Telephone: 800-379-8808
Fax: 818-986-3408
Website: www.mwp.com.

Qui Fait Quoi. Qui Fait Quoi Inc. Published Annually, Montreal, QC. Reference guide that lists media outlets in Quebec with detailed listing of television broadcasters.
Telephone: 514-842-5333
Fax: 514-842-6717
Website: www.qfq.com

TV Canada. Qui Fait Quoi Inc. Published Annually, Montreal, Quebec. Lists the key players in the Canadian Television Industry.
Telephone: 514-842-5333
Fax: 514-842-6717
Website: www.canadashow.com

Index

A & E (US), 170, 224
A & E/Canal D (QC), 170
   (Canadian Production Fund)
ABC Australia, 193
A Channel Drama Fund (CA), 159
Aboriginal Filmmaker's Program (AB), 185
Aboriginal Media Arts Program, 180
Aboriginal Peoples Television Network.
   See APTN
ACCESS-USA, 224
Access-The Education Station
   Access Alberta, 119, 159-160
ACIC (French program's) (BC), 185
   (Aide au Cinema Independent Canada)
Acquisitions, 88, 171
AFDP, 160
   (Alberta Film Development Program)
AIN American Independent Network, 224
Alberta Film Development Program.
   See AFDP
Alberta Foundation for the Arts, 160
Ancillary rights
   multimedia, 96, 100
   radio, 96, 100
   versioning, 95, 98
Andalucía TV (Spain), 212
Animal Planet (US), 224-225
APTN (NWT), 178
   (Aboriginal Peoples Television Network)
   (was TVNC)
ARD Das Erste (Germany), 204

ARD/BR3 Bayern 3, 204
ARD/HR Hessischer Rundfunk, 204
ARD/MDR Mitteldeutscher Rundfunk, 204
ARD/NDR, 205
ARD/ORB, 205
    Ostdeutscher Rundfunk Brandenburg
ARD/RB Radio Bremen, 205
ARD/SFB Sender Freies Berlin, 205
ARD/SR Saarländischer Rundfunk, 205
ARD/SWR Südwest Rundfunk, 206
ARD/WDR Westdeutscher Rundfunk, 207
Arena TV (Australia), 193
ARTE–France, 199
ARTE Deutschland, 207
Arts Councils, 54
        See Funding Bodies.
Astral Programming Fund (QC), 179
Audience
    ratings, 58, 85
    relations, 7, 49
Australia Television, 193
AVRO The Netherlands, 216

Bank financing, 62, 118, 143, 146, 189-192
Bank of Nova Scotia (ON), 189
Banque Nationale de Paris (QC), 189
Barna Alper Productions, 137
BBC 1 & 2 (UK), 218
BBC1 Northern Ireland, 209
BBC Knowledge (UK), 218
BBC Midlands (UK), 219
BBC North (UK), 219
BBC Prime (UK), 220

BBC1 Scotland, 219
BBC South (UK), 219
BBC1 Wales (UK), 219-220
BC Arts Council, 157
BC Film, 157
BC Film Incentive Tax Credit, 60, 100, 140, 157
BC Heritage, 157-158
BC Production Financing Program, 157
BC Project Assistance for Media Artists, 157
BC TEL New Media and Broadcast Fund, 158
BCTV, 158
Bell Broadcast and New Media Fund (ON), 179
Betacam camera, 19
Books, television budgets, 22
Bravo! (Canada), 150
Bravo! Fact (CA), 150
Bravo USA, 225
British Columbia Cultural Services, 157
British Columbia Film, 157
Broadcast license, 5, 63, 71-78
Broadcasters
    American, 63, 146-147, 224-229
    cable, 150-229
    Canadian, 47-88, 51, 144-145, 150-178
    educational, 55, 159, 165, 170, 173
    exclusive rights, 76-77
    first window, 49, 76
    foreign, 63, 146-147, 193-224
    internet, 7, 77, 89, 135
    license, 5, 71-79
    mission statement, 11
    national, 48-51, 144-145, 150-157
    non-exclusive rights, 76-77
    private, 152, 184, 198
    provincial, 51-52, 145, 157-178

public, 150-229
   regional, 158-223
   second window, 52, 76
   website, 7
BRTN TV1 & TV2 (Belgium), 176-197
Budget
   cuts, 148
   determining your, 9-11
   long form, 21-21, 42-44
   top-sheet (short form), 20, 41
   template, 22

Canada Council, 179-180
   Aboriginal Media Arts Program, 180
   Grants to Film/Video Artists, 180
   Grants for First Productions, 180
Canada/Newfoundland Cooperation Agreement
   on Cultural Development, 174
Canada/Nova Scotia Cooperation Agreement
   on Cultural Development, 174
Canadian Audio-Visual Certification Office.
   See CAVCO
Canadian Broadcast
   Program Development Fund (BC), 187
   Production Fund (CA), 170, 187
Canadian Broadcasting Corporation.
   See CBC
Canadian Centre for Philanthropy, 56
Canadian Certification Number, 77-78
Canadian Directory to Foundations, 56
Canadian financing, 59
Canadian Heritage, 56, 181-182
Canadian Film/Video Production

Tax Credit Program. See CAVCO
Canadian Independent Film & Video Fund.
  See CIFVF
Canadian International Development Agency.
  See CIDA
Canadian Multi-Culturalism Program.
  See Canadian Heritage
Canadian Radio-television &
  Telecommunications Commission.
  See CRTC
Canadian Retransmission Collective, 97
Canadian series, 154
Canadian Studies & Youth Programmes, 182
  Part of Canadian Heritage
Canadian Television Fund.
  See CTF
Canal + (France), 200
Canal + Belgique (Belguim), 197
Canal + Espana (Cal Sur), 213
Canal + Finland, 198
Canal + Horizons (France), 200
Canal + Norway, 211
Canal + Sweden, 214
Canale 5 (Italy), 210
Canal D (QC), 170, 172-173, 179
Canal Famille (QC), 172
Canal J (France), 199
Canal Jimmy (France), 200
Canal Vie (QC), 170-171
CanWest, Global (CA), 152
CanWest Global Development Fund (ON), 182
Carlton Television (UK), 220
Case studies, 8, 106
CAVCO, 60, 180
  (Canadian Audio Visual Certification Office)

CBC, 46, 119, 132, 139-140, 150
    (Canadian Broadcasting Corporation)
CBC affiliate stations, 161-162, 167-168
CBC Maritimes, 175
CBC Newfoundland, 174-175
CBC Newsworld, 138, 151
CBC strands, 151
CCV Canal Communitat Valenciana, 213
    (Canal 9 TVV)
CD Rom rights, 77, 96, 100
CFCF (QC), 171
CFCN-TV (AB), 160
CFCN Production Fund (AB), 160
CFPL (ON), 167
CFQC-TV (SK), 166
CFRN-TV (AB), 117, 161
CFRN Production Fund (AB), 161
Channel 4 (UK), 220
Channel 5 (UK), 220
CHAT-TV (AB), 161
CHEK-TV (BC), 158
CHEX (ON), 167
CHUM-(ON) City affiliate stations, 167, 169
CICI/CKNC (ON), 167-168
CICT (AB), 161
CIDA, 182
    (Canadian International Development Agency)
CIDO, 163
    (Manitoba Cultural Industries
    Development Office)
CIFVF (ON), 117, 176, 183
    (Canadian Independent Film & Video Fund)
Cinefocus Canada, 111
CISA (AB), 161-162
CITY TV (ON), 168

CIVT-TV (BC), 158-159
CJCH (ATV/ASN) (NS), 175
CJOH (ON), 168
CJOH Development Fund, 168
CKCO (ON), 168
CKPR/CHFD (ON), 168
CKRD (AB), 162
CKSA (AB), 162
CKVR (ON), 169
CKY (MB), 161
Cogeco Production Program (ON), 183
Cogeco Program Development Fund (ON), 183
Comedy Channel Australia, The, 195
Comedy Network, The (Canada), 152
Commitment letter, 68-70
Contact information, 234
Contract
    broadcaster, 22, 62, 68-72, 75, 78
    distributor, 86-91
Copyright, 16-17, 35
Corporate sponsors, 58
Cover letter, 33
Cover page.
    See Title Page
Craig Broadcasting, 164
Crew, 20-21
CRTC, 77-78
    (Canadian Radio-television
    Telecommunications Commission)
CTF (Canadian Television Fund) (ON), 183
CTV affiliate stations, 158, 160-161, 166-168,
                        171, 175
CTV Saskatchewan, 162
CTV Television Inc. (CA), 46, 152

Deal memo, 68
Deferrals
    crew, 61, 109
    director, 45, 61
    editing facilities, 61
    equipment houses, 61
    producer, 24, 45, 60-61
    suppliers, 61
    wages, 61
Demo tape, 29, 67
Denmark DR TV, 197
    (Danish Broadcasting Corporation)
Denmark-TV2, 197
Denmark-TV3, 198
Director, 19, 29, 60-61
Director of programming.
        See Programming Director
Discovery UK, 221
Discovery Channel Australia, 193-194
Discovery Channel(Canada), 5, 46, 98-99, 152
Discovery Channel US, 99, 225
Distribution
    non-theatrical, 89-90
    theatrical, 87-89
    types of, 85-87
Distributors, 48, 63-64, 77, 86-95,
Dr. Geoffrey R. Conway Programming Fund, 186
Draft Script, 25
DW Deutsche Welle (Germany), 207

Educational
    distribution, 85, 89
    facilities, 63, 86
    rights, 77

English language version, 95, 98, 133
English programming, 178-179, 185
Enterprise P.E.I., 175
EO The Netherlands, 216
    (Evangelical Broadcasting Corporation)
ETB (Euskal Telebista), 213
    ETB1 & ETB2 (Spain)
Expenditures
    above-the-line, 20-21
    below-the-line, 20
    contingency, 21
    indirect, 21
    labour, 59
    post-production, 20-21, 24-25, 45, 118, 127, 134

Family Channel, The (Canada), 153
FAP (Filmmaker Assistance Program (CA), 185
Federal tax credit, 59-60, 100, 119, 133, 140, 180
FFC Fox Family Channel (US), 225
FIDEC (QC), 171
    (Financière des Entreprises Culturelles)
Filmmaker Assistance Program.
    See FAP
Film New Brunswick, 175
    NB Film tax credit, 175-176
Finance plan, 4, 22-24, 32, 34, 79
Finance reference guide
    American broadcasters, 224-229
    Canadian national
    television broadcasters, 150-156
    Canadian provincial
    television broadcasters, 157-178
    Foreign broadcasters, 193-224

interim financing, 189-192
national funding bodies, 179-188
provincial funding agencies, 157-178
Financière des Entreprises Culturelles.
See FIDEC
Financing
banks, 62, 118, 143, 189-192
equity, 184, 187
interim, 62, 146, 171, 189-192
self, 3
sources confirmed, 23-24
sources unconfirmed, 23
Finland-Canal +, 198
Finland-MTV3, 198
Finland-TV, 198
YLE TV 1 & YLE TV 2
First draft, 74
First Projects Film & Video (ON), 169
First window, 49, 76
Focus
idea, 11-12, 149
project, 17-18, 36
statement, 12
Foreign films, 154
Foundation funding bodies.
See Funding Bodies - foundations
Foundations, 55-57
France 2, 200
France 3, 200-201
French language version, 95, 98, 119, 133
French program's Aide au Cinema Independent
Canada. See ACIC
Funding bodies
arts councils, 54, 56, 79, 145, 157, 163, 165,
169-170, 176-177, 179-180

foundations, 55
government, 15, 27, 47-48, 53, 56, 60, 66, 79-80,
        95-98, 110, 114, 132, 145-146, 148,
        157, 160, 163-166, 169, 170-187
industry, 53
interest groups, 57
national, 146, 179-188
non-profit, 27, 53, 55
organizations, 22-23, 27, 53-57, 68, 75-76, 92, 97,
        114-115, 146-148
private, 4, 21, 45, 53, 64-66, 99, 158, 160, 166-167,
        170-171, 179, 182-189
provincial, 145, 157-178
public, 4, 21, 53, 171
sponsors, 58
Fundraising, 2, 4, 80, 98
Fundy Communications Program
    Development Fund (ON), 176
Fundy Community Television (NB), 176

Gala Films, 131
Government (Also see Funding Bodies)
    branches, 56, 66, 114
    funding agencies, 53
Grampian Television (UK), 221
Granada (UK), 221-222
Grants
    for aboriginal artists, 180
    for documentaries, 163, 186
    for first production, 169, 180
    for production, 157, 160, 163-165, 169
    to film/video artists, 169, 180
    to media artists, 157, 165, 180
    to new media, 179

Hallmark Entertainment Network (US), 225
Heritage conservation, 56
HGTV Canada, 153
    (Home & Garden Television)
HGTV USA, 225-226
    (Home & Garden Television)
History Channel, The, UK, 221-222
History Channel, The, USA, 226
History Television (Canada), 46, 153
Home video
    market, 89, 99
    rights, 77, 89, 99
    sales, 89, 96, 99
Horizon Learning Channel (Australia), 194

IKON, 217
Income, 53, 62, 85
Incorporation, 73
Independent Film Financing (ON), 189
Independent producers.
    See Producers
Independent Production Fund.
    See IPF
Industry funding bodies.
    See Funding Bodies - industry
In-house production, 145
Insurance.
    See Production - insurance
Interest fees, 62
Interest groups funding bodies.
    See Funding Bodies - interest groups
Interest groups, 57, 66, 99

Investments
    equity, 53, 80
    self-financing, 3
IPF (ON), 179, 184
    (Independent Production Fund)
IItalia 1, 210
ITV-UK, 133, 222
ITV-Edmonton, 162
ITVS (US), 226
    (Independent Television Service)

Kanal 5 Sweden, 214
Kennerson Productions, 120
Knowledge Network (Canada), 159
Knowledge TV USA, 226

La Chaîne Histoire (TPS) (France), 201
La Cinquième (France), 201
Legal
    contract, 78, 90
    insurance, 94
    license, 71
    litigious field, 73
Le Reseau de l'Information.
    See RDI
Le Reseau des Sports.
    See RDS
Letters of interest, 79
Letters of support, 27-28
Liability, 73, 93
License fee.
    See Broadcast-license

Life Network, The (Canada), 153-154
Lifestyle Channel (Australia), 194
Lifetime (USA), 226

Malcolm Silver & Co. (ON), 189
Man Alive (CA), 151
Manitoba Arts Council, 163
    Film/Video Production Grant, 163
    Film/Video Script Development Grant, 163
Manitoba Cultural Industries Development Office.
    See CIDO
Manitoba Film & Sound Corporation, 163-164
    Development Financing Program, 164
    Production Financing Program, 164
Manitoba Film & Video Production Tax Credit, 164
Manitoba Television Network.
        See MTN
Marketing, 58, 82, 89, 149, 165-166, 173-174
Marketing director, 121, 126
MDR Mitteldeutscher Rundfunk (Germany), 207-208
Merchandising, 96-97, 100
Mezzo (TPS) (France), 201
Mini-series, 159, 167, 183-184, 188
Mira Productions, 107
MTN, 164
    (Manitoba Television Network)
MTV3 (Finland), 198
Multiculturalism program, 181
Multi-media, 77, 89, 96
Music cue sheets, 76
Music rights, 20, 73-74, 91-92
Music royalties, 76
Musimax (QC), 171
Muzzik (France), 201-202

National Bank of Canada, 190
National cable channel, 194-228
National Film Board.
    See NFB
National funding bodies.
    See Funding Bodies-national
National Geographic Channel Australia, 194
Nederland TV1, 217
New Brunswick's Labour Incentive Film
    Tax Credit, 175
Newfoundland & Labrador Arts Council, 176
Newfoundland & Labrador
    Film Development Corporation, 176
Newfoundland & Labrador Film Tax Credit, 176
Newsworld strands, 151
NFB (QC), 184-186
    (National Film Board)
Nickelodeon (US), 227
Nine Network (Australia), 194-195
Nova Scotia Arts Council, 177
Nova Scotia Film Development Corporation, 177
Nova Scotia Film Industry Tax Credit, 177
NRK1 (Norway), 211
NRK2 (Norway), 211
NT: Assistance for Artistic Projects (NWT), 177

Odyssée, La Chaîne Documentaire, 202
    (TPS) (France)
Odyssey Channel (USA), 227
Odyssey TV (Australia), 195
OFDC, 169
    (Ontario Film Development Corporation)

OLN (Canada), 154
    (Outdoor Life Network)
OLN (USA), 227
    (Outdoor Life Network)
Ontario Arts Council (OAC), 169
    Artists' Film & Video Grants (ON), 119, 169, 180
Ontario Film Development Corporation.
    See OFDC
Ontario Film & Television
    Tax Credit Program, 60, 119, 169
ONTV, 169
ORF1 & ORF2 (Austria), 196
Organization funding bodies.
    See Funding Bodies - organizations
Outdoor Life Network.
    See OLN
Ovation, The Arts Network (US), 227

Pay Movie Channel, 166
PBS (US), 227-228
    (Public Broadcasting System)
Perpetuity, 91
Planète (CSN) (France), 202
Premiere (Germany), 208
Prequels, 101
Pre-sales, 64, 88
Press kit, 84
Press release, 83-84
Prime TV (CA), 154
Private funding bodies.
    See Funding Bodies - private
Producer
    business aspect, 2-3

co-producer, 26, 63, 133
creative aspect, 2-4, 12, 19, 74, 91
experienced, 10, 21-22, 26, 144, 146
independent, 49, 52, 145, 151
investment, 24
new, 10, 17, 25-26, 78, 89, 106
selling yourself, 65
Production
    aspect of financing, 1-2
    financing program, 13
    insurance, 21, 72, 94
Production schedule
    delivery, 24-25, 45, 67
    post-production, 24-25, 45
    pre-production, 24-45
    schedule, 4, 24-25, 45
Programming department, 49
Programming director, 14, 49
Promo tape, 28, 32
Promotional costs, 87
Promotions, 28, 72, 82-83, 94
Proposal
    binding of, 14-15
    budget, 20-22
    cover letter, 33-34
    finance plan, 4, 22-24, 79
    originality, 8-9
    presentation, 14
    producer's resume, 25-27
    production schedule, 24-25, 45
    project focus, 17-18, 36
    resumes, 46
    sample documents, 14, 33-46
    story synopsis, 18, 37-38
    story treatment, 19, 39-40

title page, 15-16, 35
writing of, 2, 4, 11-12, 14
Pro Sieben (Germany), 208
Provincial funding agencies.
    See Funding Bodies - provincial
Provincial tax credit, 59-60, 145
Public Broadcasting System. See PBS
Publicity
    advertisements, 87, 94
    brochures, 6, 94
    end credits, 75
    flyers, 87, 94
    magazines, 83,
    newspapers, 83, 85, 148
    photographs, 84, 94
    promotions, 82-83
    radio programs, 83, 96

Quebec Refundable Production Tax Credit
    Program, 171, 173

Radio Canada, 154, 173
RAI Uno (Italy), 210
RAI Due (Italy), 210
RAI Tre (Italy), 210-211
Ratings, 58, 85
RDI (CA), 154
    (Le Reseau de l'Information)
RDS (QC), 172
    (Le Reseau des Sports)
RDTV (AB), 165

Release forms, 51, 72-73
Republic National Bank (ON), 190
Resources, 7, 89, 144, 230-237
Retransmission
  collectives, 97, 100
  rights, 97
  royalties, 97
Rights
  ancillary, 94-98, 100
  CD Rom, 77, 96, 100
  educational, 77
  exclusive, 76, 87, 90
  home video, 77, 89, 99
  multi-media, 77, 96, 100
  non-broadcast, 77
  non-exclusive, 76-77
  non-theatrical, 88-91, 94, 97
  retransmission, 97
Rogers Documentary Fund (ON), 186
Rogers Telefund (ON), 186
Rough cut, 74
Roughcuts (CA), 151-152
Royal Bank (CA), 190-191
RTBF (Belgium), 197
RTÉ1 & Network 2 (Ireland), 209
RTL 2 (Germany), 208
RTL 4 & RTL 5 (Netherlands), 217
RVU Educatieve Omroep, 217
  (Educational Network-Netherlands)

S2, Scottish Media Group (Scotland), 222
S4C Welsh Fourth Channel (Scotland), 222
Saskatchewan Arts Board, 165

Media Arts Grant, 165
Saskatchewan Communications Network.
   See SCN
Saskatchewan Cultural Industries, 165-166
Saskatchewan Film Employment
   Tax Credit, 166
Saskatchewan Program Development
   Fund, 162, 166
SaskCulture Cultural Assistance Program, 165
SaskFILM, 166
   Saskatchewan Film & Video Development, 166
   Scriptwriters Fund, 166
SBS 6 (Netherlands), 218
SCN, 165
   (Saskatchewan Communications Network)
Scottish Television, 223
Scriptwriters Fund, 166
Second window, 52, 76
Sequels, 101
SF1 (DRS) (Switzerland), 215
SF2 (Schweiz 4) (Switzerland), 215
Shaw Children's Programming Initiative (AB), 186
Shaw Television Broadcast Fund (AB), 186
Showcase Television (CA), 154
Single-purpose company, 73
Sky Travel (UK), 223
SOCAN, 76
   (Society of Composers, Authors & Music
   Publishers of Canada)
Société Developpement des Entreprises Culturelles.
   See SODEC
Société Radio-Canada (QC), 173
SODEC (QC) , 172-173
   (Société Developpement des Entreprises
   Culturelles)

Space: the Imagination Station (CA), 155
Specialty channels, 5, 48
Spin-offs, 101
Sponsored funding bodies.
   See Funding Bodies - sponsors
Sports Network, The.
   See TSN
Step-up fee, 92
Stills, 84, 94
Subtitle, 95
Superchannel (AB), 166-167
SVT1 & SVT2 (SVT Sweden), 214-215

Tax
   credit, 59-60
   foreign, 92
Telefilm Canada (QC), 183, 186-187
Telepool (Germany), 208
Tele-Quebec, 173
Teletoon (Canada), 155
Télétoon (TPS) France, 202
Télévision Quatre Saisons (QC), 173
Ten Network (Australia), 195
Téva (TPS), 203
TF1 (France), 203
TFO (ON), 170
   (TVO French-language network)
The Learning Channel.
   See TLC
3sat (Germany), 207
Title page, 15-16, 35
TLC (The Learning Channel) (US), 228
Toronto Arts Council, 170
Toronto-Dominion Bank (CA), 191-192

TNT (US), 229
  (Turner Network Television)
Travel Channel, The, UK, 223
Travel Channel, The, USA, 228
Treehouse TV (CA), 155
TS1 Switzerland, 216
TSN (CA), 155
  (The Sports Network)
TSR Switzerland, 216
Turner Network Television.
  See TNT
TV1 Australia, 195
TV2 Denmark, 198
TV2 Norway, 212
TV3 Denmark, 198
TV3 New Zealand, 196
TV3 Norge (Norway), 212
TV3 Sweden, 215
TV3 Televisíon de Catalunya, 213-214
  (TV3 & Canal 33) (Spain)
TV4 Sweden, 215
TV5 Canada, 173-174
TV5 France, 203
TVA (QC), 174
TVE1 & TVE2 (Spain), 213
TV Finland, 198
TVG Spain, 214
  (Companía de Radio-Televisíon de Galicia)
TVNC (NWT), 178
  (Television Northern Canada)
TV Norge, 212
TV NZ New Zealand, 196
TVO French-language network.
  See TFO
TVOntario, 170

UTV (UK), 223

Versioning, 95
VideoFact, 188
Vision TV (CA), 155
Voyage (CSN) (France), 203-204

Websites, 7, 53-54, 148
West coast, 145
WIC Entertainment (CA), 158, 161, 165-167,
                              169, 188
    (Western International Communications Ltd.)
Witness, 151
Worldwide rights, 91
WTN (CA), 156
    (Women's Television Network)

YLE FST Finland, 198
YLE TV1, 198
YLE TV2, 198
YTV (CA), 156

ZDF Zweites Deutsches Fernsehen, 209